WHEN HELL FROZE OVER

OVER

WHEN HELL FROZE OVER

OVER

◆

THE MEMOIR OF A KOREAN WAR COMBAT PHYSICIAN WHO SPENT 1010 DAYS IN A COMMUNIST PRISON CAMP

William Shadish, M.D.
with
Lewis H. Carlson

iUniverse, Inc.
New York Lincoln Shanghai

WHEN HELL FROZE OVER
THE MEMOIR OF A KOREAN WAR COMBAT PHYSICIAN WHO SPENT 1010 DAYS IN A COMMUNIST PRISON CAMP

iUniverse books may be ordered through booksellers or by contacting:

iUniverse
2021 Pine Lake Road, Suite 100
Lincoln, NE 68512
www.iuniverse.com
1-800-Authors (1-800-288-4677)

Because of the dynamic nature of the Internet, any Web addresses or links contained in this book may have changed since publication and may no longer be valid.

The views expressed in this work are solely those of the author and do not necessarily reflect the views of the publisher, and the publisher hereby disclaims any responsibility for them.

Cover Graphic: AMEDD Museum Foundation, San Antonio, Texas

ISBN: 978-0-595-46899-7 (pbk)
ISBN: 978-0-595-70758-4 (cloth)
ISBN: 978-0-595-91188-2 (ebk)

Printed in the United States of America

This book is dedicated to all the brave men who died in the North Korean prison camps and to my wife Karen, our children, and our grandchildren.

Out of the night that covers me,
Black as the pit from pole to pole,
I thank whatever gods may be
For my unconquerable soul.

In the fell clutch of circumstance
I have not winced nor cried aloud.
Under the bludgeonings of chance
My head is bloody, but unbow'd.

Beyond this place of wrath and tears
Looms but the Horror of the shade,
And yet the menace of the years
Finds and shall find me unafraid.

It matters not how strait the gate,
How charged with punishments the scroll,
I am the master of my fate:
I am the captain of my soul.

—William Ernest Henley, *Invictus*, 1875

Contents

List of Illustrations

A TRIBUTE TO DOC SHADISH

Tadashi "Dick" Kaneko

○ ○

(Sfc. Kaneko was an operation and intelligence NCO with Head-quarters Company, 8th Cavalry Regiment during the Korean War. He first met William Shadish when both were prisoners of war.)

Dr. William Shadish is an unsung hero for former Korean War POWs. We owe him our gratitude and appreciation for his unselfish professionalism, dedication, and humanitarianism, especially as applied to the enlisted ranks.

Doc, as we called him, was the only American physician who remained in the enlisted men's compound in Camp Five during the most difficult period of our prison experience. All the other doctors were either dead, disabled, or separated by the Communists. Because Camp Five was the largest camp, Doc certainly attended to and counseled more prisoners than did any other doctor, and he did this with whatever means or medicine he could beg, borrow, or steal from our captors.

Doc came from the 2nd Division, an outfit that suffered heavy casualties, so he was a legend even before I met him at the so-called hospital on the hill in Camp Five, where I lay incapacitated from April to October 1951, a survivor of the Russian experiments with chicken and pig tissue implantations. One of his medical staff members, Sgt. Charles Schlicter, told me about Doc's no nonsense approach and acts of raw courage in Death Valley, where our men were dying daily from starvation, disease, and exposure to below zero weather.

Doc was a big man, whose mere size and demeanor commanded respect. We always viewed him as a soldier, as well as a doctor, because he demanded that everyone adhere to sanitation and discipline. Unfortunately, because he had so little medicine or equipment, he practiced sheer force of will and mind over matter when treating his fellow prisoners. Because of him, many of us survived when it would have been so easy just to have given up.

Doc himself has been very much affected by the physical and emotional after-effects of starvation, diseases, and the lack of any medical supplies or equipment in camp. He laments the high mortality rate the prisoners suffered, which exceeds that of any World War II experience. He carries a heavy burden of those who died, especially the young, who could not cope with the adversities of that first winter of 1950–1951. His prison experience remains a vivid picture, including those nightmares that are so familiar to all of us. To Doc, it seems only yesterday that these events took place.

For Doc Shadish's bravery as a soldier and his unwavering patriotic and humanitarian ideals, both during and after the Korean War, he deserves, at the very least, the Distinguished Service Medal. Better still, would be the Presidential Medal of Freedom for his life long support and advocacy for POW rights.

No one has had a greater impact on the lives of POWs and their families than Doc Shadish; yet, he is a very humble person, who never brings attention to himself. He makes no self-serving speeches or writes articles extolling his exploits in the prison camps. However, he has written valuable medical articles that many former POWs have used to advance their cases to health care providers and government agencies. In addition, as a member of the Veterans Administration's Advisory Committee on Former Prisoners of War and as a private citizen, he has personally assisted hundreds of former POWs with their military or POW disability claims. Because of his advocacy, compassion, and personal intervention, Doc Shadish is considered the healer of Korean War and POW wounds.

FOREWORD

Lewis H. Carlson

o o o o o o o o o o o o o o o o o o o o o o o o o o o o o o o o

Dr. William Shadish is a great American! He should have received the highest medal that this country has.

—Sfc. Harley J. Coon, Past National President of the Korean War Veterans Association and the National Korean War Ex-POW Association

In August 2003 I had the privilege of speaking to a group of soldiers at Fort Lewis, Washington, about what it meant to be a POW during the Korean War. I had just published a book titled *Remembered Prisoners of a Forgotten War*, and some of the men who survived this horrific ordeal were sitting in the audience. At the end of my remarks, a two-star general asked, "Based on your POW work, who are your heroes?" The question took me by surprise. Anyone who works with former POWs always wonders how he would have reacted to incarceration, so I said, "Anyone who survives, is a special hero of mine." But then I amended my comments: "If forced to be specific, I would choose the captured American doctors who had to care for their men in those bleak North Korean prison camps, under the most intolerable of conditions. However, hero may be the wrong word. After all, John Wayne, Frank Sinatra, and many other Hollywood actors played war heroes without ever having served in the military. Following movie scripts that bore little resemblance to reality, such roles often reduced heroic acts to the level of the banal; hence, I prefer to say I stand in awe of those physicians who, without sufficient medical supplies, clothing, food, or shelter, had to make life and death decisions regarding the treatment of their fellow prisoners, more than half of whom would not survive their first year in captivity.

◆   ◆   ◆

Despite the fact that at least two out of every five Americans captured during the Korean War died in captivity, the survivors remain the most maligned victims of all American wars. For more than a half century, military leaders, the media, and even scholars described literally hundreds of these former prisoners as "brain-washed" victims of a heinous enemy or, even worse, as "turncoats" who betrayed their country. In either case, those accused apparently lacked the "right stuff" America expected of her brave sons. The most notorious reinforcement of this condemnation appeared in the well made but badly distorted 1962 film, *The Manchurian Candidate*, but many lesser films, countless novels and short stories, myriad news accounts, and even scholarly treatises perpetuated this negative image. Especially devastating were the publications of journalist Eugene Kincaid and U.S. Army Major William E. Mayer, both of whom accused an entire generation of young Americans of lacking bravery, character, and patriotism.

Unfortunately, the views of these critics received much more attention than did the refuting words of five U. S. Army physicians, who were themselves POWs. Majors Clarence L. Anderson and Alexander M. Boysen and Captains Sidney Esensten and Gene N. Lam, joined Captain William Shadish in challenging Kinkead and Mayer's contention that perfectly healthy American POWs simply gave up and died:

> The erroneous impression has been created that prisoners of war who were in good physical health gave up and died; this is not true. Every prisoner of war in Korea who died had suffered from malnutrition, exposure to cold, and continued harassment by the Communists. Contributing causes to the majority of deaths were prolonged cases of respiratory infection and diarrhea. Under such conditions, it is amazing not that there was a high death rate, but that there was a reasonably good rate of survival.[1]

As has been true in all our wars, there were those few POWs who were guilty of gross misconduct and even collaboration, and twenty-one prisoners did refuse

---

1.   Major Clarence L. Anderson, Major Alexander M. Boysen, Capt. Sidney Esensten, Capt. Gene N. Lam, and Capt. William R. Shadish, "Medical Experiences in Communist POW Camps in Korea," *Journal of the American Medical Association*, Sept. 11, 1954, 121. The entire text of this article can be found on page 124 in the Appendix.

repatriation. The vast majority of prisoners, however, simply tried to survive under the most intolerable of conditions. And their conduct, rather than manifesting personal or societal weaknesses, as their critics charged, was far more likely to reflect the changing conditions of their captivity.

◆   ◆   ◆

Americans, programmed as they are by their popular culture, know precisely how prisoners of war are supposed to react. The fictional POWs of the silver screen, whether William Holden in *Stalag 17* and *The Bridge on the River Kwai* (World War II), Ronald Reagan in *P.O.W.* (Korea), or Sylvester Stallone in *Rambo* (Vietnam), always waged incessant war on their dim-witted captors, escaped when possible, sabotaged and killed when necessary, while always retaining their purity of line and commitment to God and the American way of life. In reality, it is much more difficult to predict how men will react after becoming prisoners of war. Sometimes it is indeed the bigger than life individual who performs heroically, but more often it is someone of more common carriage who rises to the occasion. John Wayne was a fictional character, created by Marion Morrison, who became the archetypal American hero. Audie Murphy was unimpressive in both appearance and as an actor, yet he was the most highly decorated American soldier of World War II. The same kind of comparison might be made between Sergeant Alvin York of World War I and Gary Cooper, who played him in the movie. Hollywood does not create heroes for the real world; rather, it is military exigencies that inspire ordinary men to perform heroic deeds. Without question, Dr. William Shadish is such a man.

Bill Shadish could never manifest the imposing physical swagger of the Duke or the frenetic intensity of Rambo. He also does not possess the heart-throb good looks of a Gary Cooper. What he does have in abundance, however, is courage. He also has a quiet but commanding demeanor and exemplary intelligence and medical skills. In addition, he is an unblushing patriot, with an unyielding sense of duty. Bill Shadish, who received two Purple Hearts, is, as one of his fellow prisoners described him, "A man's man!" No one, however, will learn any of this from the man himself; Bill Shadish is far too modest for that. But the men who know him best, those who were with him in combat and in the prison camps, readily testify to his greatness.

Sergeant Paul Miller, who served as a medic under Captain Shadish, recalls his great courage and intensity in combat:

Bill Shadish is my hero. I first met him in August 1950 at the 2nd Battalion aid station in the Pusan perimeter. The North Koreans were shelling refugees, and someone brought in a little boy who had his arm blown off. It was just hanging by a thread of meat. Doc Shadish cleaned up his arm, and then went outside the tent and shook his fist toward the north and began screaming.

I also remember that he refused to leave the wounded the day before he was captured, until ordered to do so by his commanding officer. I can still see him a few months later in a temporary camp called Death Valley, saying goodby to those prisoners who were healthy enough to leave for Camp 5. Bill had chosen to stay behind and continue to care for those who were physically incapable of leaving.[2]

Stanley "Sam" Davies, who was a British Army Chaplain with the Royal Army Chaplains' Department, describes an incident that also illustrates Bill Shadish's courage:

One day we were all crowded into the lecture room in Camp 5 to discuss our opinion of the Chinese's so-called "Lenient Policy." No one volunteered to speak. For some twenty minutes there was a deadly silence. The Chinese were furious. They called on Dr. Shadish to stand up and give his opinion. He stood stolidly in absolute silence. The guards removed him to the camp headquarters for a grilling of several hours. Bill was ordered to confess his "hostile attitude" and to admit that most American prisoners who died in that first grim winter of captivity died of syphilis and venereal complications brought on by their sexual misconduct. Bill steadfastly refused to assent to this lie, and would not sign any document. After much abuse and bullying, he was returned to the compound with a severe warning. We all greatly admired Bill's brave and steadfast conduct. His cheerful, calm, and philosophical attitude in these wretched POW camp days were a tonic for us all.[3]

Paul Dowd, who was a field artillery first lieutenant when captured, admired both Bill Shadish's courage and his ability to do so much with so little in Camp 5, which was the largest of the North Korean prison camps:

Bill was the resident doctor for the enlisted compound in Camp Five. He did have his medical pouch, although there was nothing in it. He held sick call every day. Most of the people had diarrhea or dysentery or pneumonia or some other god-awful disease. Bill would give a lot of advice because that's about all he had to work with. He was there for quite awhile, but then

---

2.   Telephone interview with Lewis Carlson, May 10, 2004.
3.   Letter to Lewis Carlson, April 16, 2004.

rejoined us in the officers compound in Camp 5, where he was not allowed to practice any medicine. He was liked by everyone, and he was a man you could trust. The line Bill drew in the sand was far out in front of the rest of us. He was a very tough guy, and very principled.[4]

Sergeant Robert Fletcher, who after the war was to serve with Dr. Shadish on the Veterans Administration's National Advisory Committee for Former POWs, agrees that Bill Shadish was a caring man, but he also admires his inner strength when having to make life and death decisions concerning the very sick:

> Doc Shadish is one of my heroes. I met him when he was making the rounds in Camp Five to help guys who were sick. The compassion he had for these guys was just unbelievable. He would almost break down because there was nothing he could do for them, other than comfort them. The Chinese gave him some white powder. I'm not sure what it was, but he had to make a choice of giving it to those who were already dying and those who were just sick. He was forced to make decisions on who had a chance to make it and who did not.
>
> He was always so cool under pressure, and his personality is still the same as it was then. He was warm and very outgoing and always tried to do the best he could under intolerable conditions. He didn't even have an aspirin he could give the men. But he would never tell a person he was going to die. He would always encourage them to get up and get their strength back, and that's all he really could do.[5]

Sgt. Harley Coon, who later served as National Director and President of the Korean War Veterans Association, admired Bill Shadish's talents as a physician who was often forced to treat his patients with nothing more than kind words, but he also recalls his bravery when they were first captured:

> December 1, 1950 was the day many of us were captured. The Chinese had closed the escape routes from the Kunu-ri area. Dr. Shadish, without fear of his life, stayed to care for the wounded of the 2nd Infantry Division who were trapped. Bill Crawford told me that the Chinese threatened to shoot him if he continued to care for the wounded. Dr. Shadish ignored their warning....
>
> After we reached Camp 5, I came down with wet beriberi, yellow jaundice, and pellagra. There was another soldier by the name of James Coughnour who had the same diseases. Dr. Shadish came to our hut to check on the sick and wounded. He told Jim Coughnour and me not to work or do anything. Jim

---

4. Telephone interview, May 13, 2004.
5. Telephone interview with Lewis Carlson, May 12, 2004.

Coughnour went on a rock carrying detail. When he came back that night, he looked very sick. During the night James Coughnour died. Dr. Shadish could only give you verbal suggestions because he had no medicine. If Dr. Shadish gave you advice, and you took it, you had a chance to survive.[6]

All the men who knew Bill Shadish support Harley Coon's contention that he "should have received the highest medal that this country has." Yet, even a man of Bill Shadish's heroic stature and noteworthy accomplishments initially came under suspicion, however groundless, when he returned home. In this he was no different from the other 4,000 POW survivors, who were interrogated about alleged misbehavior and collaboration in the prison camps. Hopefully, this memoir will help set the record straight, and not just for Bill Shadish, but for all these men who suffered so much, not only at the hands of the North Korean and Chinese Communists, but from their own government as well.

◆   ◆   ◆

A note on methodology and sources: On two separate occasions I spent several days audio-taping Bill Shadish in his beautiful Northern California home. There were also countless followup telephone calls. Fortunately, he has a near photographic memory, and the result of these interviews was a typed transcription of more than 100 pages. In addition, over the years he has filled several notebooks with his recollections. He also kept copies of his many reports, articles, speeches, and correspondence relating to his more than three years as a combat and POW physician. Finally, under the Freedom of Information Act, he was able to obtain his government file, part of which included a long and extremely detailed account of his POW experiences that he put together for military authorities in January 1954 while convalescing at Walter Reed Army Medical Center. His government file also contains the particulars of the U.S. Army's investigation of his loyalty, an investigation that was as pointless and humiliating as it was unnecessary for one of the true heroes to emerge from the Korean War.

Lewis H. Carlson
Austin, Texas, August 2007

---

6.   The first paragraph of Harley Coon's recollections initially appeared in "The Gray-beards," January-February, 2003, p. 4. The second paragraph is from a May 22, 2004 email sent to Lewis Carlson.

PREFACE

Over the years, family and friends have urged me to put on paper my observations as a physician who endured life and death in the North Korean prisoner-of-war camps between December 1, 1950 and September 5, 1953.

I knew that I should write such a memoir, but somehow I always found excuses to delay. Part of my procrastination was undoubtedly due to a deep-seated reluctance to relive painful memories of the 1010 days I was held captive by the Communists. But time and tide wait for no one, and I did want Americans to learn of the duplicity and cruelty of those Communist regimes, for whom the end always seemed to justify the means.

There is much about the Korean War POWs that is either distortion or simply untrue. For example, officially there were 7,140 American prisoners, 2,701 of whom died in captivity. This is a 38 percent fatality rate, which approximates the death rate of Americans held by the Japanese in World War II. However, our actual fatality rate was much higher than 38 percent. There are officially still 8,177 Americans listed as Korean War MIAs, and certainly many of these men were prisoners, although never reported as such by the Chinese or North Koreans. I would argue that our overall POW fatality rate was more than 50 percent and between 65-75% for that first winter of our captivity. In addition, these deaths were not accidental but due to deliberate deprivation, dehumanization, and a lack of care for the sick and wounded.

I also want readers to understand that the widespread indictment of our Korean War POWs was based largely on distortions, misinformation, and personal agenda. I am particularly referring to books such as Eugene Kinkead's *In Every War But One* (1959) and Raymond Lech's *Broken Soldiers* (2000), the reports and articles of U. S. Army psychiatrist William E. Mayer, and the syndicated columns by Col. David H. Hackworth, all of which concluded that the majority of us were guilty of gross misbehavior and mass collaboration with the enemy and that somehow our high death rate was our own fault.

Above all, I want to relate what transpires physically and mentally to prisoners of war when forced to live under conditions beyond the grasp of human imagination.

ACKNOWLEDGMENTS

Above all, I thank my wife Karen, without whose writing and computer skills and loving support this book would have remained an unfulfilled commitment.

I am deeply indebted to my fellow prisoners of war who shared their experiences so freely and who gave their heartfelt support to this project. I especially want to single out my medical corpsmen and Dr. Gene Lam, who provided indispensable aid to me and the other prisoners in Death Valley and elsewhere.

I am very grateful to Lieutenant General Leonard Heaton, who as Surgeon General of the Army afforded me many meaningful military assignments.

All former Korean War POWs owe a debt of gratitude to Albert D. Biderman, the author of *March to Calumny*, and to those twenty-one prominent social scientists, who in the early 1960s supported us when men such as Eugene Kinkaid and Major William E. Mayer sought to convince the American public that we were collaborators whose astronomical death rate was due to our personal moral and psychological shortcomings.

Mr. Philip A. O'Brien, who is the Department of Defense's expert on POW/MIA affairs, provided invaluable research help, as did Ms. Billie White, the librarian at the Mercy Medical Center of Redding, California, who located numerous articles on diseases related to vitamin deficiencies.

Special thanks go to iUniverse's Nick Neary, Eric Kingery, and Kristin Oomen for all their help and encouragement.

Finally, and especially, I want to thank my coauthor Lew Carlson, who has worked so hard to put together this account of what happened to our men in the prison camps of North Korea. I first learned of him through his numerous books on World War II and Korean POWs. His understanding of what transpired in the camps is exceptional. He has become a trusted friend whom I admire. His thoroughness, encouragement, and consistent search for truth and accuracy have made the dream of this book become a reality.

NORTH KOREAN POW CAMPS

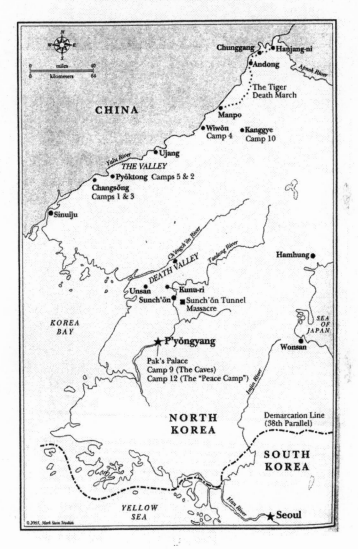

1

BEGINNINGS

The lessons I absorbed during my formative years helped me survive combat, being a prisoner of war, and life itself. Early on, I learned to be self-sufficient, yet do my share for the entire family. Because it was the Great Depression and we were very poor, I understood that we all had to work, and work together, or none of us would make it. I also learned that you can endure the hardest of times if you are determined to do so. From my mother I learned compassion, respect for all human beings, and the power of religion. From my father, I learned hard work, perseverance, and to hate communism. From both, I learned honesty and to embrace the strength of the family as a working unit.

◆　　◆　　◆

I was born on May 16, 1924 in Bridgeville, Pennsylvania, about eight miles south of Pittsburgh, the youngest of thirteen children. My parents had emigrated from what had been part of the old Austro-Hungarian empire, but is now Slovenia, in northern Yugoslavia. My father was born Jacob Cadiz, but his name was changed to Shadish in 1895 because the immigration officer at Ellis Island thought that's what Cadiz sounded like in English. My mother's name was Elizabeth Strauss. She arrived in 1900, the year they were married. My parents were among the millions of immigrants from Southern and Eastern Europe who came to the United States in the late 19th and early 20th centuries seeking a better way of life. They arrived without money or a word of English, but willing to do anything to survive.

My father was a tall, quiet man. I didn't get to know him all that well, because he was always working in the coal mines near Bridgeville. He went to bed early because he had to get up at 4:30 to make it to the mines on time. I can remember him coming home from work so covered with coal dust that he was almost black.

1

Mother would fill up a big tub in the kitchen with hot water and scrub his back and head.

With thirteen children, Mother got up as early as Dad. She was very small, maybe five feet tall, and nobody was more lovely, kind, and gentle. One incident truly describes her. When I was twelve or thirteen, a beggar came to the house who had obviously been drinking. He asked for money for a meal. All we had in the house was maybe fifty cents, but my mother gave him a quarter. I said to her, "Mom, you understand he's going to take that money and drink it up." She gently replied, "Son, that's his sin, not mine." That was my mother.

Our house was right by the bus stop. It had beautiful roses in our front garden, and when businessmen returning home from Pittsburgh jumped off the bus, they would ask, "Liz, how about giving us a rose?" And she would always give them one. When she died, her funeral was one of the largest our town had ever seen because everybody knew and loved her.

My mother and father were good, honest, and wonderful parents, who worked so hard for so little. They spent their entire lives trying to pay off the mortgage on our old, two-story, wooden house. Downstairs were a kitchen, a small livingroom, and a back room which at times was used as a bedroom. Upstairs there were two bedrooms. The boys slept in one and the girls in the other. We pumped our water from a well, until, when I was a teenager, we finally got indoor plumbing.

The Shadish home, circa 1920s

Mother and Father Shadish

The Shadish family in 1907, seventeen years before Bill was born. From left to right: Anna, Elizabeth, Jack (standing), Frank (sitting), Jacob, and Mary

As a boy, I knew nothing about my grandparents, other than that they were farmers back in Slovenia. Until 1940, my parents received occasional letters from them. These were not cheerful letters, and it was clear that their lives were very hard. After 1940, we heard nothing more, except that they had joined the Chetniks, who fought under former Yugoslav Army Colonel Dragoljub Mikhailovich against the German occupation. When my mother read in a Slovenian newspaper that the Germans had caught and executed Mikhailovich, she was so upset that she cried for him, just as she had for Emperor Franz Joseph when he died.

In 2003, my wife Karen and I went back to Yugoslavia to find out about my family. We discovered that my mother's family had a dairy farm. I didn't succeed in finding my father's family, but the last day in Sophia Locha I saw a big truck with the name Cadiz on it. I talked to the driver and discovered he had a meat-packing business that delivered to grocery stores. Apparently, there were a lot of Cadizes in Slovenia, but we were unable to track down my father's family before we had to leave.

Our parents insisted that their children speak English, and they were right, because we had to assimilate. My older siblings could also speak Slovenian, but by the time I came along the younger ones spoke only English. My brothers and sisters all respected education, but because money was so tight only two of them went to college. Agnes graduated from Slippery Rock State Teachers College and became a teacher. Frank was also very intelligent and ambitious, and, in many ways, the mainstay of our family. During the day he worked in town at a chemical factory called American Cyanamide, and at night he attended Carnegie Tech in Pittsburgh. It took him thirteen years, but he got his degree in chemistry. I would often go into Pittsburgh with him. He'd drop me off at seven in the evening at the Carnegie Library and Museum. I would stay there until eleven when he would pick me up to go home. I loved to read, and those wonderful hours spent studying the museum exhibits triggered my life-long interest in rocks and fossils.

Frank bought our family its first automobile in 1934. It was a 1932 Chevy, which was a car you could work on yourself. We had a garage with a cross beam and a pulley, and I can remember helping him hoist up that engine, changing piston rings, and repairing anything else that needed fixing. Then in 1935 Frank bought a new Ford, which was the biggest thing in our lives up to then.

Three of my siblings died before I was born. The oldest was Martin, and my mother, who never got over his death, cried every time she thought about what happened to him. In those days they pasteurized milk by boiling it on the stove. He was a toddler about three years old. He reached up, and pulled down the boiling pot, and burned himself so severely he died. She always blamed herself for his death. Two of my sisters died during the 1917 flu epidemic. My oldest surviving sibling was Jack, who worked in the steel mills. Mary was my oldest sister. She married a coal miner. Most of my sisters worked as domestic help. My sister Frances worked in a Jewish grocery store, owned by the Abramowitzes, who were very kind to her. They also gave me a job on weekends stoking their furnace.

Because we were from the Austro-Hungarian Empire, we were called Hunkies, which was a derogatory name. Our parents' reacted to this kind of discrimination by insisting that we had to prove ourselves. They told us, "Get an education, work hard, and show them you are not a Hunky," and we did.

We had several ethnic groups in Bridgeville, but there was very little intermingling. There were large Italian and German neighborhoods. The Slovenians lived next to the black section of town, which meant, of course, we had mostly black neighbors. They were good, wonderful people. I remember the Adamses, Hostons, and Milners lived across from us, and we kids played together. In times of bereavement our families tried to help each other, and color did not matter.

The mine workers were mostly Slovenians and Italians, although there were also a few blacks. The men also worked in steel mills, the closest of which was in Carnegie, about four miles from Bridgeville, where I worked after I graduated from high school. Unfortunately, because of the Depression, coal miners and steel workers were often without jobs. I can remember times being so miserable that my father's take-home pay for two weeks was fifty cents, and we had to live on that.

To help make ends meet, my mother took in boarders. She also had a garden, in which she grew corn, potatoes, and tomatoes on the half-acre of land that we had behind the house, but her speciality was strawberries. We would box them up, and I would walk a mile up to what we called "Bank Property," where I sold them to the bankers, lawyers, and businessmen who lived there.

Every time any of us made some money or my father got paid, we would sit around the table and mother would say, "Bring me the bills." There was always a grocery bill. She would insist we pay off our bills, and if any money was left over, we could perhaps then buy something for ourselves. That's a philosophy that has stuck with me to the present day. I don't like credit card buying, because doing so can often get one into financial difficulty.

Next to our house was the Oeschlegers' slaughter house and grocery store. We kids used to watch the Oeschleger boys butcher cattle. Once a year our family bought a pig. We would kill and boil it, rub the hair off the hide, and then skin it. We used everything but the squeal. We even used the intestines for sausage casings. Dad had a six by six foot smoke house where he smoked the hams and sausage, which we then stored in our basement. This at least provided us with a little meat during the rest of the year. However, one pig for a family of twelve did not go very far. Mostly we ate potatoes. During the really bad times, we ate one or two potato patties, and that was it.

Our garden out back had a depressed area that flooded when it rained. When I was sixteen, my dad said, "I have a present for you." It was a wheelbarrow. A block from us they were building a new road, and there was lots of dirt to be had. All that summer I wheeled dirt back to our house. That helped built up my strength and toughened me up for playing football at Lincoln High School.

Right guard Bill Shadish is third from the left.

My parents were Roman Catholics, and religion became very important to me. Bridgeville only had a couple thousand people, and we Catholics all went to St. Barbara's Church. Dad wasn't that religious but mom certainly was, and she insisted that her children go to church every Sunday. It was a mile and a half walk, and bitterly cold in winter. As a youngster I was turned off by this gruff, old, bantam-rooster priest we had, who clearly believed the way to present Christianity to the young was to frighten them into obedience. I figured I was condemned to hell forever. Fortunately, I developed a much different understanding of the church and Christ's teachings as I grew older.

When I was a prisoner of war, I spent a lot of time in the punishment hole because I was always getting into trouble. That was the hardest time to endure because you were in solitary confinement under extremely bad conditions, and you were never quite sure you would get out alive.

You had nobody to talk to, so you had lots of time to think about God. My entire life I had recited the 23rd Psalm: "The Lord is my Shepherd, I shall not want…." When I repeated the 23rd Psalm over and over again, I no longer felt alone, and that really helped.

The Communists were active in Bridgeville during the Depression. They wanted to unionize the miners, who were not then organized. My father very much opposed unions because he thought they were a communist idea. I can remember my brothers and brothers-in-law patrolling our yard with rifles at night because Communists were burning down the houses of those opposing the union. I remember one night when a loud explosion woke me up. Just down the street, the house of a man who had publicly criticized the union was on fire.

I attended the public schools in Bridgeville. I always received good grades at Washington Elementary, mostly because of the head start my sisters gave me. I always said I had eight mothers, seven of whom were my sisters. They mothered me to death, and I was undoubtedly the most spoiled of all my siblings. We all had to work and do our share, but they doted on me. They taught me everything they learned, so before I even started school I knew the alphabet, could read and write, add and subtract, and much more.

Lincoln High School offered three educational tracks: academics, business, and vocational. I especially liked science and math, but I was quite sure I would be a laborer. Even so, I dreamed that one day I might be able to go to college, so I chose the academic track. For practical reasons, I also spent three nights a week attending the Mesta Machine Shop School in Pittsburgh, learning to be a machinist.

After I graduated from high school in 1942, I got a job working as a machinist at the Superior Steel Company in nearby Carnegie. Within six months I had been promoted to night supervisor, which meant I was deferred from the draft because we were working on big naval guns. My high school friends, however, had all gone off to war, and I felt a sense of guilt about not being with them. So on February 13, 1943, I volunteered for the service. I told the Army recruiters I wanted to go into the artillery because I could use my math, and they agreed.

My father died in 1941. He was still working in the mines, although he was then seventy-two. He had been suffering stomach problems, but we did not have a very good doctor. Although my father was in great pain, the doctor told him not to worry about it except that he shouldn't drink so much. Like so many of the miners, when dad had the chance, he would buy a pint of whisky. Then one day dad went into the bathroom and vomited pure blood. We took him to a hospital in Pittsburgh, and he died three days later from cancer of the stomach.

My oldest brother Jack died at eighty-eight. When Jack was maybe fifty, he married a woman who liked to dance. She was a good-looking woman, and he was very much in love with her. Coming home late at night from a dance they were driving down a hill and a milk truck pulled out in front of them. Jack had driven race cars, so he tried to get up on the sidewalk and miss the truck. He couldn't get the second wheel up and he hit a telephone pole. He was paralyzed on one side of his body and never fully recovered, but he never lost his spirit. He kept saying, "I'm going to get better one of these days." He finally got a job working in Pittsburgh as an elevator operator. His only way to get there was to walk the eight miles, although usually someone would pick him up because everyone knew "Old Jack."

My mother died in 1946. I don't remember her getting any social security after my father died, but we kids were able to help some. I received $32 a month in the army, and I would send $16 home to mom, and live on the rest. Of course, one didn't have many expenses in the service, other than for beer and partying, and I did neither. Frank also helped support her, as did my sister Agnes. What I didn't know until after mom's death was that she had saved every penny of that $16 a month I sent her so she could give it back to me when I came home from the service.

2

FROM U.S. ARMY ENLISTED MAN TO MEDICAL OFFICER

U.S. Army recruit William Shadish, May 1943

On February 13, 1943, I was inducted into the army and took my basic training at Camp Swift, just outside Austin, Texas. Near the end of basic training, we all took some kind of intelligence test. The good Lord works in marvelous ways, and four of us were selected to go to college to study engineering. This was wonderful news for me because it was something I had wanted my entire life. We were briefly assembled at Louisiana State University with about thirty other selected soldiers from other camps and then assigned to different schools. Several of us ended up at Pittsburgh's Carnegie Tech, where my brother Frank had graduated, and only ten miles from home.

This was the ASTP Program (Army Specialized Training Program), and I studied basic engineering. They packed almost two years of normal college engineering courses into nine months. It was intense, hectic, and stressful, but I enjoyed it. At the end of the nine months, we each received a week's leave. After we returned, we had to take another test. On the test was a drawing of a skull, with various nerves and arteries labeled mostly in Latin. They then took away the original and gave us the same drawing with the names eliminated and told us to write them back in their proper place. I had taken Latin in high school, so this was easy for me. Again, four of us were selected to attend either medical or dental school, and they asked us our preference. I told them that I really preferred to stay in engineering and wanted to be transferred to a combat unit. At the time, I had little desire to be a physician or a dentist; what's more, it bothered me that I had not seen any combat. Nevertheless, I was told, "You will go to pre-med and then medical school, and that's an order!" I later realized how fortunate that order was.

My assignment was to Syracuse University for pre-med classes. Once again it was nine months of intense study, after which I was supposed to have the equivalence of a Bachelor's degree. I again enjoyed the hard work and had no problems academically. I was supposed to start medical school in the fall of 1945, but I still thought I wanted to be an engineer.

While waiting for my assignment to medical school, I was stationed at the Staten Island Army Hospital as a surgical technician in the operating room. This was an enlightening experience, but I was still not that excited about medicine when I began my medical studies in September at the Long Island College of Medicine in Brooklyn. I was also a little unhappy that some of the others had been sent to Harvard, Yale, and other more prestigious sounding schools. However, I later discovered that the Long Island College of Medicine had an excellent reputation.

Initially, I was not as serious about my medical studies as I should have been, but this changed after I was put on the wards. Moving from the theoretical to the practical really inspired me, but then I had to work like the devil to catch up.

In December 1945, I was discharged from the service, but fortunately the G.I. Bill allowed me to complete my medical studies at the Long Island College of Medicine. I received $65 a month from the government, as did my three room-mates, Bill Hoopes, Leo Jivoff, and Hal Lueders. We rented a room in a boarding house for $25 a month, cleaned it up, and purchased cheap bunk beds. Each of us also put in $25 a month for food. We bought blocks of cheese, bread, and lots of noodles and made our own meals.

I received my medical degree in June 1949. By then, I also had a wife and son. I had met a nurse my junior year, and my strict religious upbringing did not allow me to play loose with women. I had been taught if you started going out with a girl, you better be thinking about marriage, so I married Mary Jane McDermott in 1948. We were blessed with our son William, Jr. the following year and our daughter Mary Elizabeth the year after that. As a result, when I was ready to start my internship, I had a new family but no money, and my internship was only going to pay $25 a month. I had little choice, so I decided to go back into the army, which at least paid me a living wage.

After re-enlisting in the U.S. Army Medical Corps, I began my internship at Kaiser Permanente Hospital in Oakland, California. Permanente was an excellent internship, but it was Kaiser's first pre-paid hospital plan, and many in the medical profession did not approve, as I discovered when I went before the examining board to obtain my California license to practice medicine. I was wearing my army uniform, and the examiners asked me where I had interned. When I told them Permanente, I could tell by the frowns on their faces they were upset. I finally did get their approval, but only after one of them asked, "Why are you here if you are working at Permanente?"

I finished my internship on June 30, 1950. If things had been normal, I would have paid back my internship time, and then probably left the service. At the time, I saw myself becoming a general practitioner somewhere back east and working closely with civilians. But just five days before I completed my internship, the Korean War broke out. On July 1, I was ordered to report to Travis Air Force Base in Fairfield, California, some forty-five miles northeast of San Francisco. The next day I was on a plane heading for the Far East.

3

KOREAN WAR COMBAT PHYSICIAN

Three plane loads of doctors left Travis Air Force Base on July 2, each carrying fifty physicians. I was relieved that I was heading for Korea, because I still suffered guilty feelings about not having been in combat during World War II.

Now, at last, I felt I would be doing my share. We landed in Hawaii and stayed overnight at the Royal Hawaiian. The next day we flew to Wake Island and then on to Tokyo. Once again, it seemed like four was my magic number. Four of us were taken off the planes in Tokyo and told that we would be staying in Japan.

I was assigned to the 35th Area Station Hospital in Kyoto, the most beautiful city in Japan. It was a small, general hospital, with only one other physician. The two of us divided up the services: I was to be chief of surgery, responsible for the surgical services. He was chief of internal medicine and pediatrics.

We lived on the top floor of the hospital, and every day an old Japanese woman cleaned our room and washed our clothes. At the end of my first week, I asked my fellow officer, "What do I pay her?"

He replied, "A chocolate bar."

I said, "You're kidding."

He insisted, "No. She will take the chocolate bar on the free market and be one of the wealthiest people in her neighborhood. We don't want to disturb the local economy." I didn't think much of his comment.

I stayed in Kyoto about four weeks. It seemed like an ideal place, but once again I began to feel a sense of guilt. All my friends were going to Korea, while I was again enjoying a soft assignment. In early August, Eighth Army Surgeon General Edgar Erskine Hume came to Kyoto to visit our command, which threw a cocktail party for him. I downed a couple of drinks, just enough to oil my tongue. When I met General Hume, he must have noticed my attitude. He asked, "You don't look very happy. What's the matter?"

I told him, "Well, sir, I served in World War II but did not get to go overseas. Now, once again I'm being shielded from combat duty, and I feel bad about it."

That's all it took. The next morning, an orderly awakened me at six o'clock and said, "Pack your bags and be at the railroad station at twelve o'clock. You're going to Korea."

I took the train to Tachikawa Air Force Base, where I met Gene Lam, another army physician, who would become one of my closest friends. The next day the two of us and another physician flew to Korea. We landed at Taegu, near the point of the Naktong Perimeter where our troops were in a desperate struggle for survival against the North Korean forces. We were immediately taken to the basement of an old, bombed-out building, where a Colonel DuVall of the Army Medical Corps greeted us: "I admire and envy you guys," he said. "You are going into the best experience of your lives. You're going to love it. I only wish I was going with you, but I'm too old. Now, do you have a weapon?" We did not, so he ordered us to get one.

Gene and I were assigned to the 9th Infantry Regiment. He became Battalion Surgeon of the 1st Battalion, and I was made Battalion Surgeon of the 2nd Battalion. Things were going so badly for the Ninth Infantry that it looked like the Communist forces might breach our defensive lines and push us all back into the sea. This would have resulted in another Dunkirk, such as the British suffered early in World War II.

I was assigned to head up the 2nd Battalion Medical Aid Station. Several days before, North Korean troops had overrun them, and captured their doctor. When I asked if there were any further news of him, I was told he had been found dead, hanging by his neck. I thought to myself, "Great! What have I got myself into?"

The next four to six weeks were a real education in front-line combat medicine. There was certainly nothing in my internship that could have prepared me for treating wounded soldiers, and there had been no time for any training in Korea, because the military so badly needed physicians at the front. Even if there had been time, I don't think they could really have trained us for what we encountered.

Our regimental surgeon and my commanding officer was Major Burt Coers. He was a good doctor, and I greatly admired him. Burt was Regular Army, and I think he would have rather been an infantry line officer than a practicing physician. He loved tactics, and he taught me enough about the subject that he saved my butt a couple of times. Once, when the North Koreans were breaking through our lines all along the Naktong, Burt said to me, "The first thing you do whenever you set up your aid station is to find a back way out." That night the North Koreans broke through and cut off our main road, but earlier that day Burt and I had found a back road leading out, and that saved us.

My medical corpsmen were divided into groups: there were those who were constantly in the fields of fire ready to provide immediate assistance to the wounded; there were the litter bearers who brought the wounded back to the aid station, where there were additional medics; and the ambulance drivers. All of these men worked under the most dangerous and exhausting of conditions. Those on the front lines were constantly under fire, as were the litter bearers. The aid station might be anywhere from 10 to 100 yards behind the lines, depending on the terrain, and it too occasionally came under fire. The ambulance drivers ran the constant danger of being ambushed as they tried to get the wounded back to a MASH unit (Mobile Army Surgical Hospital), some twenty-five miles to the rear. The constant physical and emotional stress was enormous; yet, these men, most of whom were draftees, performed heroically and well. Several of them were also of tremendous help later in caring for the wounded and sick after we were captured, both in Death Valley and Camp 5. They were the finest soldiers I have known, and I am so very proud of them. Without question, they have never received the recognition they deserve.

Our aid station's responsibility was to cover twenty miles of a wide, open space along the Naktong Perimeter, and it was very hairy. Our charge was to administer as much definitive care as we could and to use a triage system to determine how best to handle the more seriously wounded. This started with the front line medics who always carried morphine. The morphine came in one-half gram vials which was too heavy a dose. We told them only to give the wounded half a dose, unless the casualty was clearly terminal. At the aid station, we had antibiotics, penicillin having come into use in the military in 1943. If a wound could be treated quickly at our aid station, we did so, and, when possible, returned the man to his front-line unit. At the time, our forces were spread so thin that we needed every able-bodied soldier we could find. The more seriously wounded we tried to stabilize before jeeps and ambulances ferried them from the front lines to a MASH hospital.

Unfortunately, guerilla forces were lurking behind our lines, and we quickly learned that a vehicle with a Red Cross painted on it made a prime target. The guerillas would ambush and disable the vehicle and then slaughter everyone on board. In response, we painted over the Red Cross insignias to make them less conspicuous. To make matters even more life-threatening for the seriously wounded, the evacuation route was over primitive, bumpy roads.

I personally got back to the MASH hospitals only when I had to accompany a badly wounded patient. If it was already dark, I would sometimes stay overnight with the MASH people, who were usually very nice; in fact, sometimes they would even give me a bottle of Scotch.

In mid-August 1950, the battle for the Naktong Perimeter became so desperate that a Marine unit had to be rushed up to bolster our defensive lines. The Marines had their own aid station, but early on North Korean tanks broke through and destroyed it. Our aid station then absorbed their wounded, as well as our own, which meant we were handling more than 500 casualties a day.

Under such conditions you are so busy you don't have time to think about anything but trying to save the wounded, and there was no time to reflect on the carnage of war. It hurt, of course, to see our men shot up. My corpsmen and I knew many of them because we were attached to their units. We would recognize them coming through badly wounded or even dead, but if we were to do our jobs properly, we simply did not have time to dwell on negative thoughts. And there were very few lulls in the action when the enormity of these losses might have caught up with us.

Many of us liked the Salvation Army, but we did not care much for the Red Cross. When the Salvation Army workers showed up on the front lines, they tried to help any way they could. For the most part, the Red Cross stayed away from the front lines. I recall once when I had to stay overnight at a MASH hospital, the commanding officer told me I could bunk with a Red Cross employee in his tent. The beer companies back in the States donated enough beer so that everyone on the front lines was supposed to get one beer a day, but we never got our beer, and we wondered what happened to it. When I bunked down with this Red Cross fellow, he asked me if I wanted a beer. I told him, "I would love a beer. I haven't had one for a long time." Under his bed he had at least six cases of beer. I said, "You son-of-a-bitch. That's our beer."

The reality of war is almost always at odds with how it is portrayed in our popular culture. For example, I watched a couple episodes of the television show *MASH*, and that was more than enough. It was a ridiculous show that belittled and trivialized the real MASH people, who had no time for fun and games. They often worked sixteen to eighteen hours straight and would fall asleep on the spot when they were finished. They saw the worst cases, the ones we could not handle. They were really good people, whose awesome responsibilities never allowed them to indulge in the kinds of silly escapades depicted on television.

I remember one unfortunate tragedy that would never have appeared in any television show or Hollywood movie. The Marines were moving toward the front in their Sherman tanks, which had 90 mm, self-leveling guns. If a tank headed down, the gun automatically came up. Riding between the tanks in open trucks were South Korean soldiers. All of a sudden, we heard a tremendous explosion. One of the tanks had hit a bump in the road and accidently discharged a 90-mm shell right into the middle of the truck ahead of it that was filled with South Korean soldiers. I ran up to see what I could do, but they were all dead. There was blood pouring everywhere out of the truck. It was a horrible sight, but it was an accident. Friendly fire is not always friendly.

One could understand why there was occasionally friendly fire from our Air Force or Marine planes. The Air Force jets had to fire from higher up, but the Marine Corsairs flew in so low to give us support that we would duck our heads. Nevertheless, we loved to see those Corsairs attack the North Koreans on the ridges.

The Marines were the first to use helicopters in Korea. They would drop spotters off on the mountains surrounding the Naktong Perimeter. Occasionally, these helicopters would return and land on the relatively flat land alongside our aid station. This was the first of September, and it gave me an idea. I asked the pilot of a Bell 13-B helicopter if he might be able to attach some kind of litter basket on top of his landing gear to transport the most severely injured to the MASH hospital. He came back later in the day with a litter apparatus attached. The first to be helicoptered out was a Marine officer with a sucking chest wound. I was able to plug up the hole, but in order for him to live he had to have surgery, so we strapped him onto the litter and he was flown out. To my knowledge, this was the first time a chopper in Korea or anywhere else was used for medical evacuation.

U.S. Marine helicopter flies injured soldier to safety.

The battle along the Naktong Perimeter raged back and forth for weeks. We would push back the North Koreans, but they would counterattack and hit us again. When orders arrived for the Marines to pull out, we were upset because the battle for the Naktong Perimeter was not yet over. At the time, of course, we did not know they were being pulled out for General MacArthur's Inchon landing on September 16, 1950.

The Inchon landing broke the back of the North Korean army. Our troops crossed the Naktong River one final time, chasing the enemy as fast as we could, although we never really caught up to them. At the Han River, the North Korean forces scattered to the east, so we just kept on going. We moved through Seoul and up to P'yongyang, the capital of North Korea, where my medical group bivouacked in a two-story building close to the approach of the airport runway. The first time I looked out the window and saw the lights of a big plane coming right at me, I thought it was going to fly right into our room, but it just skimmed over the top of our building. Those planes were coming in one a minute, carrying supplies for our forces.

When we moved out of P'yongyang, the North Korean troops we had bypassed had regrouped in pockets. Some surrendered but others kept fighting. I remember seeing one North Korean soldier chained to the wheel of a heavy machine gun so he could not retreat. Nevertheless, we met very little resistance as we followed the infantry northward.

We got as far as the Chongchon River by Kunu-ri, where our military leaders made some mistakes. We were chasing down these pockets of North Korean resistance and heading straight for the Yalu, which marked the northern border between Korea and China. We thought nothing could stop us, and General MacArthur promised we would be home by Christmas.

However, we did hear disturbing and persistent rumors about Chinese troops crossing the Yalu and infiltrating our lines. On November 23, we were sitting around very upset because we had not received our Thanksgiving Day dinner, when two extremely agitated South Korean officers in civilian clothes came into our Aid Station. They were commanders of a Korean unit that had moved up to the Yalu River and had apparently been decimated by the Chinese. They wanted to inform our intelligence people that Chinese troops were now in the war. We sent them back to headquarters in a jeep, but evidently intelligence did not believe them, so nothing was done.

On November 25, an artillery unit moved into our area south of the Chongchon River and placed its 105 mm guns in a small, nearby field alongside the river. They did not post sentries because they thought the river would protect them. About 10:30 that night, all hell broke loose. The Chinese had taken off their clothes, held them and their guns over their heads, and waded the river. With no one there to intercept them, they destroyed all the guns and ran shooting toward our aid station, which we had set up in a two-room Korean hut. Our hut and several other nearby buildings were surrounded by a compound wall with a low gate framed inside the wall. Most Koreans are shorter than we are, and the top of this gate was so low that we had to bend over to get through it.

I was sleeping in my uniform. When I heard the commotion, I jumped up, pulled on my boots, grabbed my carbine, and went running out of the hut. Pow! My head snapped back. I thought I had not ducked low enough and hit the cross bar when I went out the gate. I lost my helmet and was briefly dazed and then rendered unconscious because the Chinese were throwing percussion grenades. Two of them had gone off right behind me and knocked me down. I suffered a couple of minor shrapnel wounds and a concussion. When I came to, one of the infantry officers was saying, "We've got to get out of here! Follow us!" We saw no casualties, so we were able to follow them back to our main lines.

The next day our forces retook the area, and we went back to gather up our equipment. Sgt. Ken Badke came up to me with a grin on his face, and I could see he was holding something behind his back. He said, "Guess what I've got." He showed me my helmet, which had my initials and medical insignia on it. It had a crease down the middle of the top. It was a bullet that had knocked it off my head, not the cross piece over the gate.

On November 30, our 2nd Battalion moved out and right into an ambush near the town of Kunu-ri. The South Korean unit on our right had been driven south by the Chinese, which allowed them to penetrate some ten miles to our rear. Kunu-ri was located in a box canyon that ended in a perfect bottleneck, and the only road going through the pass was just wide enough for the road and little else. Looming above the road on both sides were steep cliffs, occupied by the Chinese. A couple of tanks carrying headquarters staff made it out, but the Chinese hit and disabled the next tank, effectively blocking the road. Headquarters sent in British, Turkish, and American troops from the south to free the roadblock, but they were all turned back by the Chinese.

The 23rd Infantry Regiment to the north of us took a road directly west and made it through. I'm not sure why, but there was later a controversy over whether the 23rd actually had orders to leave. I do know that their leaving left us totally vulnerable to the Chinese forces to the north. We had approximately 100 wounded lying on stretchers in the back of four trucks, another 25 or so litter patients scattered in five ambulances, and some 150 walking wounded. I heard Burt Coers radio headquarters and ask permission to take our wounded out on the same road the 23rd Infantry Regiment had taken to safety. A senior officer on the other end told him, "No way. Just stay there."

Burt asked, "Well, what do we do now, sir?"

The senior officer answered, "It's every man for himself."

I couldn't believe it! What a terrible thing to hear when you are trapped in a fire fight.

Major Homer Hinkley, who was the senior infantry officer present, ordered us to fight our way out. I approached Major Hinkley and said, "But sir, we have a bunch of wounded here."

He answered, "I know that, but if we don't destroy the roadblock, we'll all be dead, including the wounded. I want every man to get a rifle, and that includes you medics."

I wasn't happy about this and I again insisted, "We have to stay with our wounded."

He replied, "Major Coers will stay with the wounded, and you can pick a corpsman to stay with him."

I went back to the wounded lying helpless on their litters and in the back of the trucks and told them the bad news. Sgt. Bill Crawford, who was one of my corpsmen, was among the wounded. I walked over and said, "Bill, we've been ordered to take off, but we'll come back for you. Hang on."

He looked up at me and said, "Well, I sure hope so."

Later, in Camp 5, a few of the survivors of these horrific days expressed their opinion, apparently very sincerely, that they felt they had been deserted by their commanding officers. Some went so far as to transfer this feeling of resentment even to the officers who had remained and were captured with them, stating that "given the chance, all officers will save their own skins first when the chips are down." These men had seemingly lost their respect for all officers. Just how much this affected their lives as POWs is difficult to determine, but I am certain it was not a healthy attitude to have in a prisoner-of-war camp commanded by Communists. Fortunately, it was only a small percentage of the men who allowed these bitter feelings to dominate their thinking.

Years later, after we returned to the States, all of us were angry when we learned that the 9th Regiment of the 2nd Division had been accused of cutting and running when the Chinese attacked. That was a damn lie. Any rapid movement to the rear was because of orders, not cowardice. When the line soldiers were trapped at that road block near Kunu-ri, they fought valiantly against superior fire power. They did not quit; they were basically mowed down. I was there and I saw what happened. They fought against rifle and machine guns and in the face of incoming mortars until they ran out of ammunition. Anyone who calls these men cowards has to answer to me. In my mind they were all heroes. Those who want to know what really happened should read S. L. A. Marshall's *The River and the Gauntlet*, and his description of the Battle of the Chongchon River near Kunu-ri.

The thirty-five or so of us who were left followed Major Hinkley up into the hills to try and destroy the road block. We did not get very far before we ran into machine gun fire. Everyone flattened out on the side of the hill, and remained there until morning. When it became light, the Chinese resumed firing down on us, and Major Hinkley ordered us off the hill. Several of the men were killed trying to make it down the hill, including Dr. Charley Struthers, who was shot while trying to help the wounded. Struthers was a physician with the 3rd Battalion and the son-in-law of General Crawford Sams, who was himself a medical doctor. After the war I was able to tell General Sams what had happened to his son-in-law when I met him in New York at a ceremony honoring General William Dean.

Paul Miller, who was one of my top sergeants, and I retreated down the hill and headed back toward where we had left our wounded. We never got there because we could see Chinese troops swarming all over the trucks. Capt. James C. Williams and Gene Lam later got closer to the trucks and reported that many of the wounded had been massacred, presumably with burp guns.

We tried to circle around the trucks, but when we did Paul and I ran right into the middle of a squad of North Korean guerrillas before we knew they were there. They leveled their burp guns at us and there was nothing we could do. They tied our arms behind our backs and made us kneel on the ground in a shallow depression. The North Korean soldiers were laughing as they came up and pointed their weapons at us. I knew they were going to kill us, but once I realized this was the end, I felt no sense of panic because I understood there was nothing further I could do about my fate. I said to myself, "Well, it's going to feel like somebody hit me in the head with a baseball bat." Then thoughts of my family went through my head.

They were getting ready to shoot us when out of the blue a Marine Corsair flew in right over the top of us. I looked up at him and thought, "Oh, God, he's got napalm. That's one way I do not want to die. I hope to hell he doesn't drop it here." He circled around, came back, and waggled his wings. The North Korean in charge spoke a little English, and I said to him, "That's my friend. I can see the numbers on his wings, and he has napalm. If you kill us, he's going to napalm all of you." The North Koreans hated napalm for the same reason I did. It incinerates any living thing in its target area. He said something in Korean, and his men backed off and we were allowed to sit down. But then he said, "Your plane will go away."

Thank God, every fifteen minutes or so another plane flew over us. I began to think we might make it, but then I realized that with nightfall the planes would no longer be able to see us, and we would again be doomed. I had noticed a path leading down the other side of the hill, so I turned and said to Paul, "I don't know about you, but I'm not about to sit here and be shot when it turns dark. I'm going to give it a bloody go and take off down that path. How about you?"

He looked at me for a moment and said, "Okay, Doc. I'm with you."

I told him, "When I say go, we take off down that path as fast as we can."

I was about to give the signal, when my heart fell. Up the path trotting toward us was another squad of Communist soldiers. I figured this time we were surely finished, but they turned out to be a Manchurian unit from China's Fourth Field Army, and they were real soldiers. They were large men and obviously very tough. They immediately began arguing with the North Koreans. Eventually, they turned their weapons on the North Koreans, who then backed off. I think they had been ordered to take prisoners for future indoctrination sessions. In any case, they untied us and gave us water and cigarettes. One of them even gave me a swig of liquor from his canteen.

I had pretty much pushed out of my mind my moment of capture for more than thirty years, but then something truly bizarre happened. A forest service helicopter pilot sat in my livingroom in Redding, California, looking for possible investors to build a power plant in our area. His name was Chuck Burgans, and I told him I might be interested. Toward the end of our conversation, he said, "I understand you were POW in Korea. Where were you captured?"

I told him, "Near Kunuri."

He said, "I was flying over Kunuri one day and there were these two, poor bastards tied up and about to be shot by a bunch of North Korean soldiers. We kept flying over them until it became too dark for us to see. I often wondered what happened to them."

It's hard to describe what I felt at that moment, but I know I had never experienced anything like it before in my life. The two of us had lived for thirty years in the same city and had never run into each other. I had told Paul Miller after the Chinese Manchurians rescued us from the North Koreans that if I ever met the pilot who saved our lives, I would buy him the best Scotch I could find. That night Chuck and I damn near drank the whole bottle.

4

DEATH MARCH

If you cooperate with us, we will be very lenient, but if not, we will treat you as war criminals. We call this our Leniency Policy

—*Chinese political cadres to newly captured American prisoners*

While on the front lines trying to sleep, there were many nights when I thought I might be wounded or even killed, but never did I think I might become a prisoner of war. Not surprisingly, when I was first captured, my initial reaction was, "What the hell am I doing in this place as a prisoner?"

The Chinese soldiers who took Paul Miller and me away from the North Koreans took us to a prisoner collecting area near Kunu-ri, but the details of these first few days are hazy in my mind, which I am sure was the case for most POWs. One feels numb and apathetic and cares little about what is going to happen next. In truth, we were exhausted and in shock.

At the collection center, all our medical supplies were taken from us, along with our valuables. The only medical aids I remember were crude dressings administered by the Chinese aid-man to some of the most severely wounded. After my mind began to clear, I realized that I could be of help to some of our wounded, but when I asked for permission to do so, I was turned down.

Although some newly captured soldiers were executed, such as the wounded litter cases back in the valley, the vast majority were not. We later learned, the CCF (Chinese Communists Forces) were ordered to take prisoners because their political cadres were convinced that over time they could induce some of us to become sympathetic to their cause and perhaps even become Communists.

The setup was really quite simple, but diabolical, and the Chinese had already used it on their own people. They would isolate any recalcitrant subjects in camps, where they would expose them to the weather and put them on starvation rations. Then, when the victim's situation became critical and he hovered between life and death, they would tell him that treatment depended on cooperation, by which they meant going along with their re-education programs.

The Chinese began by introducing us to what they called their "Lenient Policy for POWs." They told us, "We could have executed you, but we spared you in order for you to learn the good points of Communism. If you cooperate with us, we will be very lenient, but if not, we will treat you as war criminals." Something like this had never happened before to American prisoners of war so this was a new threat for us. They also told us how much better things would be when we reached the permanent camps. However, none of the permanent camps were ready to receive prisoners, so for weeks they marched us back and forth across North Korea before putting us in temporary camps such as Death Valley, the Mining Camp, and the Bean Camp.

On December 4, the Chinese rounded up those of us who were physically able and marched us out of the collecting center. Those who were too sick or badly wounded to walk were simply left behind. They told us that those left behind would be taken care of or even turned over to the American forces, but we never saw any of these men again, and I have no idea what happened to them.

Approximately 900 of us left the collection area on December 4. My conservative guess is that we lost at least 200 of these men during the twenty days it took us to reach Death Valley. Others thought the figure was even higher, but whatever the exact figure, we lost approximately one out of every four men who began that march. And even those who survived were so weakened that many of them died after arriving in Death Valley or later in Camp 5.

There were several marches similar to ours during the first six months of the war. Unfortunately, we do not have accurate records of those who dropped out and died. Undoubtedly, these men are among the 8,177 who are still classified as Korean War MIAs.

On our march I would guess we covered fifteen to twenty miles a day over rugged mountainous terrain in bitterly cold weather. We did not know it at the time, but we were heading into the coldest winter on record. Various government reports stated that the temperatures dropped to thirty, forty, and even fifty degrees below zero. I know the day before we were captured, Paul Miller heard from Frank "Pappy" Noel, an Associated Press photographer who would also be captured, that headquarters had told him it was then 18 degrees below zero and getting colder.

Those of us who were in better shape tried to help the walking wounded, but it took two men to aid one sick or injured man, and soon there were simply too many of them to help. When some of the men could go no farther, they just sat down on the side of the road and refused to move. A guard would drop out with them, and we would march on. Soon we would hear a shot, after which the guard would catch up with us, and we would never again see the man who had dropped out. The guards also ordered some of the wounded to be left in villages along the way, and these men we also never saw again.

Many of the men who did not do well were draftees or replacement troops who did not know each other. The Marines did better because they had been together in their units for a long time, but many of our men did not even know each other's names, which meant there was no functioning buddy system or esprit de corps. These men felt alienated, even though some of us tried to reach out to them as best we could.

The Chinese and their mostly North Korean guards always marched us at night to avoid our aircraft. We would start about five in the afternoon and march until four or five in the morning. Judging by the stars, these were haphazard marches. Sometimes we moved to the east and sometime toward the west, but mostly we moved slowly northwards. I was quite sure we marched over sections of road that we had already been on. Because the permanent camps were not yet ready for prisoners, they evidently did not know where to put us.

The Chinese had a very primitive but effective air raid alarm system. They stationed guards both in front of and behind the marchers. If they heard planes overhead they would yell something that sounded like "Fiji-lala" and then fire a series of rifle shots that would be repeated up and down the line. All of us would be ordered to lie down and not move. All lights and cigarettes had to be extinguished. This happened every night we were marched.

When it came time to rest, our guards sometimes kicked Korean families out of their huts and let us stay there. The huts I stayed in never had any kind of heat. The rooms were usually six to eight feet square, and we had to jam fifteen to thirty men into each. We could never lie down. We usually rotated standing with a sitting or squatting position. And when there were no huts, we stayed in open fields. Wherever we were, we always huddled together trying to keep warm.

Sometimes a guard would take away a prisoner's boots, and then he had nothing to put on his feet except perhaps an old shirt or some rags. We could never get lost along the trail because there was a trail of blood in the snow from those who had lost their boots. Others had snow-pacs, which were worse than leather boots. Leather boots would get wet, but they would also dry out, and air would breathe through them. The snow-pacs were rubberized, and the moisture would collect inside. When we stopped, the moisture would freeze, and a lot of those men lost their toes and feet to frostbite. The army later stopped using snow-pacs in winter weather. Fortunately, I had combat boots.

To make matters worse, the guards had a routine of marching us about four hours and then stopping for forty-five minutes to rest. We worked up a sweat and then during the rest we became terribly cold. We tried to convince them that it would be much better to march for an hour and then rest for ten minutes, but they wouldn't listen.

When we got to one of those Korean huts, I would take off my shoes and socks and put my socks under my butt to try and dry them out. I tried to tell the other men to do this, but some were so tired they did not want to do anything. We were also getting very hungry. All we had each day were a couple of handfuls of dried, partially cooked whole kernel corn. We had no utensils so we ate out of our filthy hands. This corn was simply not digestible, and it was very hard on the intestinal tract. You could see the whole kernels in your bowel movements. So we all began to lose weight and suffer malnutrition.

Water is even more important than food and we had none that was fit to drink. We ate snow to try and quench our thirst, but that is very inefficient. It also makes you feel even colder. Eventually, the men began drinking from streams, but these were contaminated, and the men came down with dysentery.

We had no paper or leaves to use as toilet tissue. We learned that an old, dried corn cob, if available, does a rough but satisfactory job. Sometimes we used unsanitary slit-trench latrines in the villages. While marching, we found any available spot we could along the road.

The Chinese issued no clothing to us, and we had never received our winter uniforms because MacArthur said we would be home by Christmas. I had one pair of cotton fatigue trousers, a field jacket and shirt of the same material, one pair of socks, a pair of boots, and a pile-lined cap with ear flaps. Some of the men had gloves, but I shoved my hands up my sleeves for warmth. A few of the men had been issued overcoats and blankets, but most had lost these while trying to evade capture. When we rested, if one man had a coat, he would wrap it around himself and a buddy just trying to keep warm and preserve body heat. All that mattered was trying to survive. That march made me hate cold weather for the rest of my life.

On December 16, they put us in a village for a couple of days, where we were consolidated with another large group. Then we begin marching again. At midnight on Christmas Eve we reached the top of a mountain. It was a clear night with lots of stars. We looked around, and it was the most beautiful sight imaginable, with snow-covered mountains as far as the eye could see. I thought, "What a place to spend Christmas Eve." On Christmas morning we marched down the mountain into the valley the Koreans called Hofong. However, because of what happened there in the next few months, we called it Death Valley.

5

DEATH VALLEY—HOFONG

Approximately 1,000 of us arrived in Death Valley on December 25, 1950, or Hofong as the Chinese called it.[1] There were already several hundred prisoners there, including a number of South Korean and Turkish POWs.[2] Four weeks later, the Chinese moved most of the men to Camp 5 at Pyŏktong, leaving behind some 300 men deemed unfit for travel. Nine weeks later, only 107 of the 300 were still alive, and when in mid-March they were forced to evacuate, only 94 of them made it to Camp 5, some of whom died shortly after arriving. The shocking thing about Death Valley is not how many men died there but that anyone survived.

◆　　◆　　◆

Located approximately seventy miles south of Pyŏktong and Camp 5, Death Valley was a narrow strip of land nestled between mountains so steep that the sun reached the valley floor only two or three hours a day. So precipitous were the sides of these mountains that the Korean farmers would have to lie on their stomachs to till their small parcels of land. An icy-cold stream and a narrow road formed the only entrance into the valley.

Death Valley was divided into two separate areas with no intercourse of any nature permitted between the two. The larger, lower camp consisted of approxi-

---

1.　The Korean name for Death Valley was Pukchin-Tarigol.
2.　The exact number of prisoners held in Death Valley is difficult to ascertain. Fellow physician and POW Gene Lam put the number at 1,100, but historian Raymond Lech estimates there were 3,000, 500 of whom died. David Polk, who gathered materials on Death Valley and other camps for the Korean War Ex-POW Association, puts the number at between 1,000 and 2,000, with 1,200 surviving. see, Lewis H. Carlson, *Remembered Prisoners of a Forgotten War*, (New York: St. Martin's Press, 2002), p. 111.

mately 1,000 men and was controlled by the Chinese; North Koreans controlled the upper camp, which contained some 600 men. Although I was limited to the confines of the lower camp, later conversations with inhabitants of the upper camp convinced me that there was no significant difference in the treatment or food in the two areas.

We were quartered in a series of adobe huts that had earlier been used by miners.[3] There were no real windows or doors, only crude openings, over which we would occasionally hang an ineffective blanket to keep out the cold. Each hut was approximately ten by twelve feet, into which were jammed at least twenty-five men. We were so crowded that two-thirds of us had to sit with our knees under our chins while the remaining one-third lay down. At intervals we would rotate our positions. Some of the huts had Korean-type floor heating, but wood was so scarce that most of our warmth came from the close proximity of each other's bodies.

At first we welcomed the straw mats on the hard dirt floors, but we soon discovered they were crawling with lice. At night, they swarmed over our bodies, hair, and even found their way into our ears, all of which made sleeping very difficult. They also crawled into the seams of our clothing. Each morning we used the buddy system to pick fifty or sixty of these creatures off of each other and then crushed them between our nails.

Scabies, or psorioform dermatitis, was even worse than lice, and it too resulted from being forced to live under filthy conditions. Scabies causes a reddened scaling eruption that is highly contagious for physically debilitated individuals living so close to one another. It is caused by female mites burrowing into the skin and creating small, threadlike tunnels into which they lay their eggs. The sores that emerge on the skin cause intense itching.

Our food was pretty much limited to cracked corn and millet. The Chinese told us each man would receive a daily allotment of 400 grams, which was approximately twelve ounces, but in reality the amount we received was closer to 300 grams, or about nine ounces. Initially, we had no way of boiling it ourselves, so the Chinese boiled it for us in a big pot. Unfortunately, they did not boil the grain long enough and it was still hard. This made it difficult to digest, and it passed through our bodies without being totally assimilated. Millet is bird feed and very difficult to swallow. It is like chewing very bland sand. We never received any vegetables or protein except for one small pig that was divided up

---

3.   This was not, however, the Mining Camp, which was another temporary camp, as was the so-called Bean Camp.

among some 1500 prisoners on January 1, 1951. We had no salt or spices, no oils or fats, and no eating utensils. We tried to force the ill to eat this food, which was difficult even for a well person to do.

The only source for water was to cut a hole in the ice that covered the slow-moving stream that flowed through the valley. Unfortunately, the stream was contaminated by a North Korean army camp upstream that had used it for latrine purposes. With no way to boil the water, we all came down with diarrhea and dysentery, afflictions so severe that forty to fifty often explosive and uncontrollable bowel movements a day were common.

There were two covered latrines that were already full when we arrived. The contents were frozen solid, and we had no picks or shovels to empty them. We asked for a new latrine to be located away from the camp, but the Chinese refused. Instead, they placed several logs over a shallow depression in the ground directly in the camp area. Even so, the men were often unable to make it that far. As a result, piles of frozen, semi-liquid bloody stools dotted the landscape. Because shovels were not available, we could not clean up these areas. It was also very difficult to muster work details and to do so required constant bickering.

Some of these unfortunate men were unable to make it out of their huts and defecated in their clothing, thus contaminating their living quarters and the other inhabitants in the room. Most had no replacement garments and no adequate way to clean their soiled clothes; as a result, some of these men threw away their trousers and went naked.

We had no soap or warm water to clean ourselves or our clothes. We were no better than cattle trapped in a filthy stockyard. Not surprisingly, diseases spread rapidly and deaths often occurred, usually in the following sequence: First the individual lost weight and strength, due to malnutrition and starvation; a lack of proper clothing and the severe winter conditions further weakened him; then he contracted dysentery, which entailed fluid loss, often fever, and a loss of appetite, which exacerbated his state of emaciation.

As the men became weaker and weaker from dysentery, malnutrition, and other dietary deficiencies, pneumonia became all too common. I recalled my medical school professor, Dr. Phillip Greene, telling us in 1945, "You gentlemen are fortunate that you will never have to treat pneumonia without penicillin." At the time, the magnitude of his words did not register with me, but they certainly did in Death Valley. Without proper treatment, a debilitated patient with Pulmonary Lobar Pneumonia means certain and rapid death. The infection of the lungs causes fluid and debris to fill in the myriad small cells in the lungs. This means air, with its necessary oxygen, cannot get in. The patient literally drowns in his own fluid. He turns a darkening gray and eventually his heart gives out. This process took three or four days in Death Valley. We pleaded with the Chinese for antibiotics, but they insisted that they had none to give us.

Death Valley was pure hell, and no one seemed to care whether we lived or died. Assessing our afflictions, 100% of us had dysentery at one time or another; 100% were suffering from severe weight loss; 100% suffered cold injury, 15% of whom suffered tissue loss; 25 to 30 prisoners developed infectious hepatitis in February 1951, and 50% of them died; 100 to 150 contracted pneumonia and very few survived; nutritional edema began to develop during the latter part of February 1951, which meant the excessive accumulation of fluids in body tissues.

Of the five U.S. Army Medical Corps doctors in Death Valley, only Gene Lam and I survived captivity. Captain Edwin Ecklund died of bilateral labor pneumonia on January 29, 1951 in Death Valley, Major Burt Coers died of pulmonary tuberculosis and dysentery on March 25, 1951, and Captain Peter Kubinek died of pulmonary tuberculosis on June 15, 1951. Although Coers and Kubinek actually died in Camp 5, their fatal illnesses began on the marches or in Death Valley.

Because Burt Coers was already very ill when we arrived in Death Valley, the ranking line officer, a Colonel Campbell, appointed me to be Regimental Surgeon. My first responsibility was to inform the Chinese that I wished to assume responsibility for the medical care of the 300 men left behind when the rest of the prisoners were moved to Camp 5 on January 22, 1951. Captain Gene Lam asked to be my assistant, and some twenty corpsmen joined us. We knew that if we had left with the first group, the Chinese would simply allow those left behind to lie there and die. The Chinese agreed, but again said they had no medications to give us.

Although we had nothing with which to treat the sick and wounded, we initially tried to care for the men in their huts, but it was so crowded that no one could go in and out without stepping on somebody. We convinced the Chinese to let us set up a hospital in an old schoolhouse that overlooked our huts. Actually, it was not so much a hospital as a place to house the dying. It contained three rooms, but only one could be heated. In this room we kept the cases of pneumonia and others who were seriously ill. In another room we placed the most serious dysentery cases, while the third housed the wounded and anyone else who was ill. The only medicine the Chinese gave us was a powder called Tannalbin that the Japanese had developed for treating diarrhea. This helped if you were able to get enough, but seldom was this the case. Instead we used charcoal when available. We had nothing else, not even fresh bandages. The only bandages we had dated back to when we were captured. We washed them in the stream and used them over and over again.

These were the worst of times, and we were losing up to fifteen men a day out of the 300 who had been left behind. Men who were sick and dying would cry out, "Help me, Doc." That really hurt, because all I could say was, "Hang on. We'll be getting some help pretty soon."

We had a small potbellied stove in the room that housed the worst cases, but the chimney did not work, so there was a thick layer of smoke floating at the top of the room. It was so smoky that Sgt. Charley Schlichter and I would make our rounds on our hands and knees. In spite of the smoke, we had to gather what little wood was available. It was always a heartbreaking task to select from the thirty to forty men who were least ill to go on these wood-gathering details. The men naturally resisted going on wood details when they felt so sick and weak. I knew a few would suffer harmful effects from such exertion, and even death, but I also knew that we all would soon be dead if nobody went because we also needed the wood to cook our meager food rations.

We used heated bricks for infections and infected wounds to localize the process. We also fashioned knives from the steel-reenforcing plates found in combat boots, which we used for incisions and to amputate toes with severe gangrene. The most important thing was to keep the ill men on their feet for as long as possible, even though seriously ill. When a man lay on the floor, not exercising, his already poor appetite diminished to nothing. Because his reserves were already so low, going without food for two to three days invariably meant death.

We continuously asked the Chinese for clothing, medicine, and more food for the sick, but we were always told there was none and that we were eating the same food they did. I later discovered this was not true. We also asked for Red Cross aid, but again they refused, insisting that the Red Cross was not needed. Finally, just before we left Death Valley, rice was substituted for corn at one of the two daily meals.

The dead and the living were often lying next to each other. Sometimes a live patient would wake up in the morning, and there would be dead bodies on either side of him. We would keep four or five dead bodies in the hospital as long as we could so we could get more rations. The Chinese did not like to come into the hospital to make their count, so they made it as quickly as they could and never noticed that some of the men were dead.

When a man died, the Chinese required that we turn in all his possessions for "safe keeping." They promised to return these possession to the U.S. Government after the cessation of hostilities, but they never did. The Koreans periodically brought up a horse-drawn cart to haul away the bodies, but we would first take the clothes off the corpses because clothing was so scarce. We would then put the dead man's aluminum dog tags in his mouth and make sure his mouth was closed so the Chinese could not detect what we had done. We hoped that one day someone would find and be able to identify these men. We also asked the Chinese if we could provide a burial detail, but they refused, saying that they would bury the bodies. In the spring of 1951, when we were leaving Death Valley, we found out what they had actually done with the bodies.

I have to bless the corpsmen we had in Death Valley. They were wonderful and worked their tails off, even though they themselves were also weak, exhausted, and sick. Sgt. Charles Schlichter was at the hospital all the time. In fact, the Chinese put Charley in charge of the hospital in an attempt to humiliate those of us who were officers. Sergeants Paul Miller and Ken Badke worked diligently with us, and there were many other corpsmen whose names I can no longer recall. We would have to carry those who were too weak to walk out of the schoolhouse to go to the bathroom. I remember Paul Miller and I doing this with Dr. Edwin Ecklund, even though we knew he was not going to make it. It was on one of these trips that he just folded up between our arms and died.

One day something happened that gave us a small ray of hope. An English-speaking Chinese officer came up to me and said, "You are a doctor. We want you to come see our commander who is very ill. Will you treat him?" This commander had supposedly been one of the heroes of Mao's 10,000 mile march.

I told him, "Sure, I will treat him. When I became a doctor, I vowed to help anyone who comes to me for help." I was particularly interested in diagnosing the nature of illnesses among the Chinese because we had to know if any of their diseases could be transmitted to us.

He took me to the commander, who was obviously in an early stage of pneumonia. I told the interpreter, "I cannot help him because you have no antibiotics."

He replied, "Well, we have sulfadiazine."

Sulfadiazine is an antibacterial sulfa drug used in the treatment of infectious diseases. I said to him, "I will treat him if you also agree to give me sulfadiazine tablets to treat my men who are sick and dying from pneumonia. When he and his commander quickly agreed, I said to myself, "Thank you, God. Now I will finally be able to treat my own men."

Although the Chinese allowed Dr. Lam and me to make our daily rounds with our patients, they ordered us to move to their area so we would always be close by. We were also fed their rations, which proved they had lied to us when they insisted the prisoners were getting the same rations they were. They were eating rice, soy beans, and even some pork. They also had salt and other condiments.

We treated the commander with eight .05 gram tablets a day for four or five days. At that point his condition improved, and he left Death Valley on a horse-drawn sled. Lam and I were then permitted to return to our ordinary quarters with the rest of the men. I took the interpreter to our hospital, showed him our forty sick pneumonia patients, and told him that I needed the sulfadiazine tablets he had promised. However, he gave me only forty tablets. I told him, "Like your commander, each patient needs eight tablets a day for at least four or five days if he is going to recover." But forty was all he would give us each day, which meant each man would receive one pill per day if we were to distribute them equally, but this would have helped no one. This reneging on our deal made me more convinced than ever that one could never trust a Chinese Communist.

I said to Gene Lam, "We've got enough tablets to cure five people. If I give everybody one tablet, I might just as well throw them away for all the good they'll do." This was the most difficult situation I had to face in the prison camps because I felt I had to play God. I decided to divide the people into three groups: Those who were so ill they were going to die in a day or two, whether or not they had medicine; those with the very early symptoms of what may or may not have been pneumonia and who might survive even without medication; and those in the middle who were in the early stages of pneumonia and might be saved. Unfortunately, there were more than five people in the middle group, so forty pills a day were not enough; hence, I had to make another decision. Gene and I tried to determine among this middle group who had done the most for their fellow prisoners and would probably do so again. In other words, who had been "givers" and who had been "takers." I selected five men and gave them the medicine. I prayed for guidance in these decisions. I do not know whether or not I did the right thing, but I also do not know what I could have done differently. Some three years later, after we had been liberated and the army was interrogating us, a couple men who had survived their stay in our hospital accused me of having sold those sulfa tablets. This was a lie, but they were bitter because they had not received any medicine.

Not long after I treated the commander, I again experienced Communist duplicity and mendacity. On separate occasions, we were visited by Communist journalists. The first to arrive was a man named Shapiro.[4] I went up to him and

---

4.   This might have been Michael Shapiro, who was an English journalist who lived in China, and served Chinese interests on the international scene.

said, "Our men are dying, and we desperately need food and medicine. Can you help us with the Red Cross?"

Shapiro very bluntly responded, "You bastards don't belong in Korea so you have no complaints about conditions."

A short time later, another white man arrived in Death Valley. I saw him strolling through camp wearing Chinese quilted winter clothing. I thought he might be on our side so I went up to him and said, "I'm Dr. Shadish. Who are you?"

He answered, "I'm Wilfrid Burchett from Australia,"[5]

He did not tell me he was a Communist, so I said something like, "These little yellow bastards are not treating us well. Our men are dying right and left and we need help. Can you get our names out so the Americans will know we are here?"

He gave me several blank sheets of paper and said, "If you sign your names, rank, and serial numbers on these pieces of paper, I will get your names out for you." We put our names on paper, which he then took. Shortly thereafter a Chinese radio broadcast quoted a letter that American prisoners had allegedly signed. No one had ever seen such a letter or even knew it existed, but they read our names and ranks, and said we had signed it. This was, of course, a lie, but it was used against some of us after we returned home. I tried to tell the American authorities that we had no idea how our names were going to be used. Once again I had learned never to trust Communists.

A Korean physician, or so he claimed, visited the camp shortly before the first exodus of prisoners. He boasted of five years training as a surgical resident in the "main hospital in Seoul." He selected four of our sick men and took them to a room in the Upper Camp to perform surgery. I was allowed to witness his "surgery." He performed two phalanges-metacarpal amputations, and two deep shrapnel fragments removals. He did wash his hands but used no gloves. He donned a white gown but no mask or cap. He used an antiseptic that appeared to

---

5.   A number of American POWs encountered Wilfred Burchett in the North Korean prison camps. Burchett, who wrote for *Ce Soir*, a left-wing Paris newspaper, toured the various camps seeking interviews with prisoners. He also conducted a long interview with General William Dean, the highest ranking UN prisoner, that was later distorted for propaganda purposes. A self-admitted Communist sympathizer, Burchett described one POW camp as a "luxury resort," which naturally infuriated the prisoners. Some POWs claimed he tried to break down their morale with false claims of UN defeats. He was also supposedly involved in the so-called "confessions" concerning alleged UN germ warfare. The Australian government eventually revoked his passport.

be a weak alcoholic solution. His technic was very poor, and there was maximum surgical trauma. He refused to use morphine sulphate, although it was available. One of the patients was a black American. The Chinese took a posed photograph of him sitting outside the room with this Korean physician who had by then put on a cap, gown, and mask, and was about to administer a hypodermic medication to the patient. As soon as the photo was taken, the patient was pushed off the chair and told to go back to the compound. Although both he and I pleaded for some medicine to relieve his pain, he received none. This photo later appeared in a propaganda booklet titled *POWs Calling*. Incidently, of the four patients treated, three eventually died of grossly infected wounds, complicated by dysentery.

The Chinese ordered Gene Lam and me to sign death certificates for those who died in Death Valley. They were supposed to turn over these records after the armistice, but I am sure they never did. I already suspected as much so I began keeping a list of Americans who died in Death Valley and later in Camp 5. I managed to find a pen and a clean piece of paper, and on December 30, 1950 I began writing down the name, rank, service number, and date of death for each man whose death I could personally verify. I knew such records would be important not only to the military but even more so to the families of the deceased.

The North Koreans and the Chinese never knew what I was doing. My secret list eventually contained the names of more than 300 men who died in Death Valley and Camp 5. I hid the list by removing my pen's rubber ink tube and placing the list of names in the cavity. The Chinese constantly warned us not to take any notes, so I kept the pen on my person at all times.

In Camp 5, I was not able to write down all of the deaths. I also had to sweat out many surprise inspections, often conducted in the middle of the night. The Chinese were searching for contraband, especially guns or cameras we might use to document the truth. These inspections usually occurred at three or four in the morning. Using flashlights, they would line us up and order us to take off everything but our shorts. Because they were so puritanical, they did not want to see us completely naked. Men would hide things under their testicles or in their rectum. I kept my pen in my pocket, and when an inspector would spot it, I would protest loudly and tell him that this was a gift from my deceased mother and that it only had sentimental value. I would say, "Go ahead and try it. You'll see that it doesn't even write." Thank God, no one ever decided to open it.

Above is a partial list William Shadish kept of those who died in Death Valley and Camp 5. Listed near the bottom are Burt Coers and Edwin Ecklund, two physicians who served with Shadish.

After liberation, I gave my list to military authorities, and asked them to make a copy for me. I know the government used my list to notify next of kin because over the years I received many calls and letters from families seeking loved ones who were listed as either MIA or whom they knew died in Korea. If their names were on my list, I could help these families achieve closure. Their heartfelt gratitude made me realize that it was well worth the risk I took maintaining the list. One such person was Dr. Peter Kubinek's wife whom I talked to in Chicago after the war. It was a painful experience for both of us, but she appreciated learning what had actually happened to Pete.

In March of 1951, I was able to convince the Chinese that if they kept us in Death Valley, not only all of us prisoners would die but they would as well because of the extremely unhealthy conditions. I explained that when it began to get warm, and all those frozen piles of feces thawed, we would be living in a cesspool of deadly bacteria, and no one would survive. They accepted this and on March 12 we all left for Camp 5.

At the time, I did not know where the Koreans had taken all the men who had died that first winter. I thought they had perhaps buried them, but I should have known they could not because of the frozen ground. As we marched out of Death Valley, I looked to the left and saw stacks of bodies, four or five high, with frozen arms and legs sticking out everywhere. They looked like the photographs I had seen of dead Jews in Buchenwald. If the Chinese could not have buried the dead because of the frozen ground, it would have been better to have cremated them. I have no idea what they eventually did with these bodies or if any trace of them still exists. I know of no Americans having returned to Death Valley, but I also know exactly where it is.

◆   ◆   ◆

I have tried very hard to rid my memory of Death Valley, but I cannot. I constantly see the buildings, the smoke, the filth, and the men lying there dying. I see the bodies being carried out and thrown onto that cart and then discarded in the snow. The images of all those unnecessary deaths, and our inability to do anything about them, will never leave me.

6

CAMP FIVE—PYŎKTONG

o o o o o o o o o o o o o o o o o o o o o o o o o o o o o o o o o o o o o
*That's what's wrong with your people. They teach you how to cure,
not who to cure.*

—*Kuo Tsien-tsu, a Chinese officer whose life*
William Shadish saved

A few days before we left Death Valley for Pyŏktong and Camp 5, we each received a padded cotton coat, a blanket, and a pair of tennis shoes, all too late for the men who so desperately needed them earlier. The march itself, which the Chinese said was approximately ninety miles, began on March 12, 1951 and lasted seven days. Of the 300 men left behind on January 22, when the first group left Death Valley, only 109 were still alive to begin this final march. Those able to walk helped one another. Those who could not, perhaps fifteen or so, were placed on horse-drawn carts. We marched daily, from morning to evening, covering roughly fifteen miles per day. We received approximately two ounces of partially cooked corn in the morning and another two ounces at the end of the day. We had no boiled water to make the corn more palatable. After three or four days, we were becoming weaker and weaker, and many of the men could not keep up. The Chinese guards, obviously under orders, responded by beating those lagging behind with their rifle butts. This continued until the last day of the march, when we were all picked up by horse carts.

I have a vivid memory of a black soldier on the march with hepatitis who was riding on a cart. When he died, we removed his combat boots to give to somebody who had none. The bottoms of his feet were the brightest yellow I have ever seen on a human being. His liver must have been totally destroyed. Thirteen more men died before we reached Camp 5 because they were just too weak to

40

walk or even ride, and more died after we reached Camp 5. The American POW death rate for that first year approached 75 percent.

◆   ◆   ◆

When the prisoners arrived at the permanent camps along the Yalu River, the Chinese continued the deprivations. We soon realized that their intention was to reduce each of us to an animal state, and then, when we were close to death, threaten us by saying, "If you do not do what we ask, we will not feed you, and you will die here." As one political cadre put it, "We'll bury you so deep you won't stink, and your family will never know where you are."

Many of our men were teenage draftees, who were already near death. When they were told over and over again that they were going to die in North Korea if they did not do what the Chinese demanded, what can one expect? When I hear blowhards like Colonel David Hackworth telling us that we were a bunch of cowards, I'd like to see how he would have done in Death Valley or during the first months in Camp 5.[1] I know from experience that many of those soldiers who brayed the loudest about how tough they were and how they were going to destroy the Communists when given the chance were often among the first to collapse when the going really got tough, both on the battlefields and in the prison camps. Hackworth was never a POW and had no idea what these men endured. Earlier critics such as Eugene Kinkead and William Mayer insisted that the Chinese never physically tortured anyone, but that also was untrue. Some prisoners were beaten and even killed, but usually the Chinese simply used slow deprivation, hoping that sooner or later their victims would die or come around. That qualifies as torture as much or more than any physical blow. You do not have to abuse a man physically if you can reduce him to a level wherein he has no hope or even desire to live. This was a slow torture, day after day, week after week, and the Chinese just sat back and said, "Well, either you will come around or we'll just let you die."

---

1.   In a 1995 syndicated article, retired Colonel David H. Hackworth resurrected all the myths about Korean War POWs. He wrote, "During the Korean War, many American POWs ratted on and stole the food of their fellow inmates or allowed themselves to be used for propaganda purposes." He insisted that the men he commanded in the early 1960s "would have spit in the face of the Russkies if captured," and he promised that if we did not reaffirm and reenforce the military Code of Conduct, "we can expect a rerun of the Korean War disgrace somewhere down the bloody track." Reprinted in the *Austin American Statesman*, January 20, 1995.

The Chinese Communists were convinced from the very beginning that they would be able to indoctrinate us because they had considerable success doing so with Chiang Kai-shek's former Nationalist soldiers in China, who had no hope of returning to their former lives. The Chinese, however, did not understand how radically different our two cultures were, particularly in terms of individual freedoms and economic possibilities. Above all, we knew that some day we were going home to a better life than they could ever give us.

The initial indoctrination began when we were first captured. The Chinese promised we would be treated "leniently" if we cooperated, but their tedious lectures and attempts at forced discussions did not begin until we reached the permanent camps. The Chinese deliberately attempted to destroy our adherence to our own values and loyalties and to accept theirs, a process that was eventually called "brainwashing" in the United States. This was nothing new, as the Chinese and the Russians had practiced this on their own domestic political prisoners, as well as on the citizens of satellite countries such as Hungary, Czechoslovakia, and East Germany. Years later, the FBI informed me that the experiences of these victims did not differ from our treatment in any major way. The plan was simple but diabolical. First, you inform those under your control that you only wish to help them understand the potential situation and that they will be treated well. Of course, this so-called Lenient Policy only applied if the victims agreed to cooperate to the satisfaction of their captors. If not, at least in our case, the Chinese told us we would be executed as war criminals.

This initial threat was followed by a softening up process. Starvation rations, insufficient shelter and clothing, and a lack of medicine to treat wounds or diseases made us particularly vulnerable. Punishment was also part of the process. If the Chinese were dissatisfied with your progress, they took your food away, threw you in a punishment hole, or made you stand outside in freezing weather. They also attempted to remove all military discipline among the prisoners by segregating the officers, noncommissioned officers, and enlisted men in separate compounds or camps. In doing so, they hoped to reduce us to the most primitive level of desperation. They figured that after we were starved, frozen, confused, sick, and exhausted, we were ready for their indoctrination lectures on the wonders of communism and the evils of the "warmongering" free nations.

◆   ◆   ◆

Containing approximately three-quarters of the American POWs, before
the officers and NCOs were removed in October 1951, Camp 5 was the
first and by far the largest of the five North Korean prison camps located
along the Yalu River that separated North Korea from Manchuria. It was
situated on the side of a hill overlooking an inlet of water backed up
from the Yalu River, just outside the village of Pyŏktong. The photo was
probably taken by Frank "Pappy" Noel, a captured Associated Press photographer, who was allowed to take supervised and often staged pictures in Camp 5, some of which were later used for propaganda
purposes. The basketball court in the foreground means this photo was
taken well after negotiations were underway, when the Chinese became
much more concerned with world opinion.

My time in Camp 5 can be divided into two segments: March 19 to July 19,
1951, during which I lived with and cared for the enlisted men in the lower
camp, and July 19 to October 22, 1951, when I was moved to the officers' compound in the upper camp for indoctrination sessions with the rest of the officers.

When our final group of Death Valley survivors arrived on March 19, 1951, there were more than 2,000 prisoners in Camp 5. They were broken down into six companies, including four for enlisted men of 400-500 men each, an officers' company of 120 men, and a Turkish company of 165 men.

After arriving in Camp 5, I was taken immediately to the enlisted men's compound where Dr. Andrew "Sandy" Ferrie was taking care of the men. However, he was there for less than a week when he was ordered back to the officers' compound. Dr. Ferrie was British and a good man, and during the short time we were together we shared a room and conducted sick call. He also taught me how to extract teeth.

Because of the bad diet, all prisoners were suffering from vitamin deficiencies. Among other things, they developed scurvy, which is the result of insufficient Vitamin C, and causes swelling, bleeding, infections, and ulcerations in the gums. There were little pieces of rocks in the corn and millet we ate, and when you bit down, you'd break off a tooth and expose a nerve, which led to pain and periodontal abscesses.

The men desperately needed to eat what little food we had, but they could not chew because their teeth hurt so much. In their emaciated condition, if they did not eat for two or three days, they died, so I had to extract their diseased teeth. Initially, we had no anesthesia, and you can imagine the pain of pulling teeth in a healthy mouth, let alone a diseased one. A couple of strong GIs would hold the patient, and I would grasp the tooth and extract it. In the entire camp there was only one small pair of dental forceps, which was meant to be used on children, but it was all we had. The Chinese, who had a local dentist, used it among themselves, but they would give it to me when I asked for it.

I complained to the Chinese that it was very brutal to extract teeth without anesthesia. After repeated begging and much harassing, they eventually produced several vials of a clear fluid that I understood was some kind of opiate. With a needle and syringe I would very slowly begin an intravenous injection until the patient became somewhat groggy. Then I quickly pulled the tooth. It was not ideal, but it was a lot better than using nothing. I ended up pulling between fifty and seventy-five teeth in Camp 5. Some of the men I worked on remember me pulling their teeth as a better experience than it actually was, because they were so grateful to get rid of their problem teeth.[2]

---

2.   Lieutenant William Funchess, who had two teeth extracted by Bill Shadish, later wrote, "I don't know how many teeth Dr. Shadish had pulled before becoming a POW but he worked like a real pro on mine;" see, William H. Funchess, *Korea POW: A Thousand Days of Torment* (Clemson, SC: Self-Published, 1997), p. 70.

At first I was only occasionally permitted to visit the seriously ill in their own quarters; As time went on, however, I was allowed to go more often, which gave me the opportunity to observe the living conditions of the camp. Normally, a Chinese doctor and sometimes a political honcho would accompany me to make sure I did not talk to the men about anything except their medical problems. I would point out men who were dying of starvation, dysentery, pneumonia, and vitamin deficiencies, but when I asked for antibiotics, they would always say they had none, and when I asked for more food, they insisted we were getting the same food they were, which was, of course, an ongoing lie. They also told us they could not bring in more food or medicine because the attacks of our own Air Force severely limited what they could transport. Nevertheless, they had sufficient room to bring in horse carts loaded with Communist literature, and I saw one boat loaded exclusively with large reams of paper on which prisoners were supposed to write down their political opinions.

Occasionally, I was able to slip a patient some medicine I had smuggled out of the dispensary. Unfortunately, when the Chinese discovered what I was doing, they became very angry and made sure I no longer had access to any medical supplies.

I began holding regular sick calls every day but Sunday between one and three in the afternoon. Because an average of 150 men lined up daily outside the dispensary, I was finally able to convince the Chinese to extend the hours from 11:30 to 5:30. The sick room contained a crude desk and one or two chairs, and the men were allowed in one at a time. My function was limited to diagnosis and suggested treatment. I wrote this down on a small piece of paper, which the Chinese doctor or a political cadre usually rejected or changed. Sometimes very sick men were denied urgently needed medications because they were thought "uncooperative" during the indoctrination sessions, and some of these men died. Those who were considered "good" or "progressive students" were often given large doses of medicines and vitamins for minor aliments.

We called the Chinese physicians "barefoot doctors" because they had so little formal training or basic medical knowledge. I'm not sure whether it was ignorance or politics, but they could not admit that it was insufficient food, a lack of medicine, and bad living conditions that caused all the sickness and weakness in our men. When I would tell them, "This man is too sick to go on a wood detail," the Chinese doctor would always insist, "He's not sick," and the political honcho would back him up. I learned that if I wanted to get treatment for a patient, I had to resort to diplomacy. I would begin by asking the Chinese doctor, "What do you think? Do you think he might have this kind of problem?" He would then usually respond, "Well, yes, I would say that is what he might have." You always had to make him think that he was making the decision rather than you.

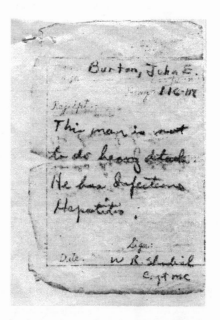

The above work release note, written by Bill Shadish in Camp 5, states, "This man is not to do heavy details. He has Infectious Hepatitis."

We had another small room for surgical work. My instruments consisted of a pair of dull scissors, a blunt scalpel, three hemostats, three finger forceps, a few bottles of a weak alcoholic solution, and small amounts of local anesthetics. We had only a half-dozen or so gauze and muslin bandages, two to three inches in width and about three feet long, which we had to wash and reuse because there were no replacements.

I recall only two or three times during the four months I was treating the enlisted men that we received a shipment of medications, and then they only lasted three or four days. A typical shipment might include 150-250 aspirin tablets, 500 sulfaguanidene tablets, 500 sulfadiazine tablets, 500 charcoal tablets, several bottles of assorted vitamin tablets, usually A or B, and three or four bottles of a bitter white crystalline powder, which was some sort of salt that the Chinese prescribed for every illness and which proved beneficial for none.

In May 1951, I was allowed to set up a sick company in the EM compound to take care of the large number of sick the main hospital could not handle. It only held 100 men. Nevertheless, this was an improvement because it made it easier for me to supervise their care. Eight American prisoners and a Turkish aid man were assigned to help out. All of us shared a small room, but we were spared the tedium of attending the indoctrination sessions.

We had no urinals or bedpans for our patients, and they had to sleep on the floor, although each was issued a blanket. I made my rounds several times daily, diagnosing and suggesting treatment. Because of the shortage of medicine, I had to practice supportive therapy, trying to keep up the patients' spirits and morale. There were also some physical things I could do, such as bandaging wounds and lancing boils and abscesses. If a man had a large, open infected wound, I would take him down to the latrine where there were lots of flies. I would remove his bandages, let the flies settle on the wound, and wrap it up again. These flies would proceed to lay their eggs in the wound, and I'd tell the soldier, "You'll be able to tell your wound is healing when it starts itching, but don't unwrap it. Wait at least a week and then we will take the bandage off." When we did finally remove the bandage, the wound would be loaded with maggots, but it would also be as clean as a whistle.

One had to improvise. The men used to call me "Hot-Water Shadish." I was forever telling them, "Just put some hot water on your affliction or go soak it." The boiling of water gave them something to do, but it also helped heal wounds because it increased the flow of blood to the area.

My greatest problem was to get the very seriously ill cases transferred from the sick company to the main hospital where more adequate food and medicine were available. Unfortunately, a man had to be near terminal to be transferred.

In June 1951, the Chinese ordered me to begin keeping medical records, which I had been asking to do from the beginning. These consisted of writing down the patient's name, rank, serial number, diagnosis, treatment, and daily observations. When I was transferred back to the officers' compound, the Chinese kept the records, but, as with the Death Valley records, I am sure no one outside of China ever saw them.[3]

During this time, the Chinese medical personnel informed us that the Russians had come up with a new treatment for illnesses. They inserted chicken livers under the skin "to prevent disease and death."[4] Obviously, this did not work, but

---

3.   A comprehensive description of the diseases Dr. Shadish diagnosed and attempted to treat in Death Valley and Camp 5 can be found on page 131 of the Appendix. He also wrote an essay on diseases related to the vitamin deficiencies the men suffered in the prison camps and a report for the Veterans' Administration on Cold Weather injuries. These can be found in the Appendix on pages 139 and 142 respectively.

the men knew if they were sent to the hospital for this operation, they would receive more and better food, and some fifty of them volunteered. The Chinese were so eager to make this work that for a week or so they fed them meat, eggs, and rice, which they would never have received normally. Every one of the wounds, however, sloughed the chicken livers.

Some of my men reported that the Chinese also administered injections to prisoners who were very ill and near death. These shots, thought to be a camphor solution, apparently contained too strong a stimulant because the effect was instantaneous, and the prisoner died shortly thereafter. The men called them "pop-out shots," because those receiving them soon "popped out" of life.

The Chinese separated the enlisted men from the NCOs in the lower camp, blacks from whites, and Turks and the British from the rest of us. Then the Chinese tried to play one group off against another. For example, they attempted to exploit racial issues to convince blacks how terrible things were for them at home. My sick call building was located just below the compound that housed the black prisoners, and I could hear the Chinese lecturing them about how whites had mistreated them and how much better they would live under communism. A remarkable black sergeant named Blue ran his compound with an iron fist. I remember hearing a black prisoner yelling at a Chinese officer, "Go fuck yourself." The officer screamed, "Who said that?" But nobody said a word. They were a good bunch and Blue led them well.

Sanitation was better in Camp 5 than in Death Valley, but by no means ideal. We dug the latrines as deep as fifteen feet, with the top breached by logs with spaces between. Once or twice the Chinese issued a small amount of lime to throw on the feces, but this did little to combat the flies, which swarmed about incessantly. The Communists also insisted on selecting the area for the latrines. They invariably located them near kitchen areas, which in the EM compounds were high on the hillside, draining down toward the well that was at the time our sole supply of water. We were, however, able to obtain sufficient firewood and pots to boil water; unfortunately, a large number of the men refused to drink boiled water because of its taste, despite the insistence of our medical personnel. Later, faucets were opened that piped water in from an unknown but healthier source.

---

4. There were also reports of using shark livers, and at least one former prisoner said he was treated with a pig liver; see Carlson, *Remembered Prisoners of a Forgotten War*, pp. 157-8.

During the several months I spent in Camp 5, I can recall receiving DDT only once or twice. Each man received approximately one ounce, but we needed much more because lice were everywhere. We tried to impress on the men the importance of delousing daily, but many of them refused, primarily because of the bitterly cold weather. As had been the case in Death Valley, it was common to see a sick man with his clothing literally covered with lice. Even if you killed all your lice every day, they were always back the next morning. Not until the end of 1952, when I was in Camp 2, did lice became less of a problem. By then, more DDT was available, we were living under better sanitary conditions, and we were able to wash and steam our clothing.

The weather in North Korea that first winter was so cold that when we breathed, the warm moisture of our breath would filter into our beards and freeze. There were always chunks of ice in our beards that we could only remove by manipulating them with the warmth of our hands.

From the time we were captured, it was close to six months before we had a chance to bathe. Naturally, we did not smell very good, but we all smelled the same. The malodorous air was the first thing we had noticed when we first landed in South Korea. The whole place stunk, and it continued to stink. To put it bluntly, the land was covered by crap-filled rice paddies, and the stench was overwhelming. Eventually, we grew used to it because of our own smelly bodies. We were filthy, with long beards and grubby hair, which also lowered our spirits and sense of well being. Finally, in the early summer of 1951, we had our first chance to get down to the river and wash. The Yalu froze over in the winter, and it took that long for it to warm up sufficiently for bathing.

We have all heard that the primary life force is sex, but Sigmund Freud was never a prisoner of war. Sex is certainly a strong drive, but in times of starvation and basic survival, food is the prime interest. During those first months, when we were starving and the death rate was so high, not once did I hear a discussion or a joke about women. Instead, we were plagued by visions and recipes of food. The men would describe in agonizing detail their favorite foods and how their mothers would prepare these delectable dishes. It was food, food, food, until someone would finally yell out, "Shut up! Enough! Go to sleep!" Without question, the prime drive in life is survival and the prime force for survival is food.

Initially, the food in Camp 5 consisted of corn and millet, but with the beginning of negotiations in the summer of 1951 sorghum was added, and the daily ration became 300 to 400 grams of grain per man per day, which was sufficient to sustain life and body weight. We also began to get small quantities of vegetables such as seaweed, squash, and daikon, and even some salt and hot peppers for seasoning. Occasionally, we received a little rice and a crude white flour-like meal for making steamed bread or dumplings, which we considered a real delicacy. The only meat we had was a small pig of less than 150 pounds to feed an entire company once every six weeks or so.

Our living quarters also improved during the ongoing negotiations. They consisted of six by eight foot rooms, initially holding six to fifteen men, which was later reduced. We got real doors and even gauze sheeting to cover the windows in an attempt to keep out the billions of flies.

We were also able to go on wood runs, and when we did the Turks found marijuana, which some of our men tried. The first time I encountered this was when I saw two blacks walking around the compound talking as loudly as they could about all kinds of things that didn't make much sense. I asked Sgt. Blue what was wrong with them. He said, "Leave them to me, Doctor." He talked to his men and got them off marijuana as much as he could. It was frightening, and I was thankful the use of marijuana did not become overwhelming.

Tobacco was also a problem. One of the most pathetic things I saw in camp, given the small dish of crappy food that we got each day, was hearing a G.I. say, "I'll give you my bowl of food for a cigarette."

I'd tell him, "If you don't eat, regardless of how bad the food is, you are going to die."

And he'd say, "I don't care."

Some of our men traded anything they could get their hands on for tobacco. Although I had never smoked before becoming a POW, I began to do so in Camp 5, but I never traded my food for cigarettes. We found tobacco along the road when we were on our wood or food-scavenging runs. The Koreans hung their tobacco on a rope to cure, and as we walked by we would grab whatever we could. Some men would sell it, but we usually shared it. In a boring situation like that smoking helped, so I began to smoke. We'd use the Chinese propaganda newspaper, the *Shanghai News*,[5] for cigarette paper.

Most people do not understand how addictive tobacco is. They think it is a habit, but it is not. It is an addiction, and a very demanding one. The tobacco we smoked in Korea was very strong, and after I came home only Lucky Strikes were strong enough for me. I did not quit until 1972.

---

5.   The *Shanghai News* was a government-approved, English-language newspaper that was made available to the prisoners, who ridiculed it because it was so filled with propaganda. In addition to using it for rolling their cigarettes, some men delighted in using it for toilet paper.

After I got home, I was often asked why more of us did not try and escape. Critics such as Eugene Kinkaid and William Mayer cited our lack of escapes to support their contention that Korean War POWs lacked courage, but, like so many of their conclusions about our alleged shortcomings, this one was also untrue. There were many men who successfully escaped, but all did so immediately after capture or during the marches when they were still relatively close to the UN lines. I also thought of escaping while being marched, but my obligation as a doctor to stay with my men took precedence.

It is true that no one successfully escaped from the permanent camps, but we had at least 200 men attempt to do so. Every day the Chinese would fall us out for roll call to determine if anybody was missing. One man was out twenty-eight days and almost made it to the ocean, but there was no realistic chance for any of us to be successful. In our weakened condition we did not have the strength to navigate the mountain paths that in winter were all but impassable. We also could not walk anywhere in the daytime without being spotted. We were white, and we walked differently than Orientals. Caucasians bounce when they walk. Orientals walk with bended knees because they so often carried heavy loads on their shoulders or heads. An escapee also could not carry enough food, so eventually he would get so hungry he would leave the mountains and go down into the villages to look for food. Any civilian who spotted a Westerner was so frightened that he immediately turned him in.

We did not discourage people from trying to escape, unless they were not well. We would even give them part of our rations. When they got caught, they were brought back to camp and usually thrown into the punishment hole.

Learning how to survive was the most important lesson every POW had to absorb. The first thing was to say to yourself, "No matter what it takes, I'm going to survive. I know it's going to be tough, but I've been through rough times before, and I'm going to make it." If you felt sorry for yourself and started moaning and groaning and constantly complaining about your situation, you simply made yourself more vulnerable. Anger against the Communists and all they had done to us could also help fuel one's determination. After all, no one wanted to be buried in that godforsaken land. There were, of course, lethal wounds and diseases you could not control, but I am talking about the mental part of surviving.

If you were a religious person, you had to reaffirm your faith. I knew that no matter what the Communists did, they could never dislodge my religious beliefs. When you felt all alone and up against something you feared you could not handle, you needed somebody by your side. Every time I was thrown into the punishment hole, I recited the 23rd Psalm, "The Lord is my Shepard, I shall not want...." I would go through the entire Psalm and then repeat it over and over again, which always comforted me.

I also learned to share, to do my part, and to take the hard stuff in stride. We had to support and work together as much as possible, but friendship could be a tricky thing. If you got too close to someone, and he died, it could be devastating, especially if your own mental state was fragile. Our 9th Medical Company consisted of approximately 150 men. We knew and worked well with each other. But the line troops, after losing so many men, did not always get to know their replacements, many of whom were captured shortly after arriving in Korea, and this made a difference in their willingness to support and help one another. Nevertheless, I would try to get the healthier men to aid those who needed it the most, such as helping them go to the bathroom, sharing blankets with them, or even talking and showing an interest in them. This kept them busy and provided a needed psychological boost for all involved.

It was also important to remain physically active, and many of us regularly walked around the compound. Later, in Camp 2, when the Chinese allowed it, some of us also became active in sports.

Finally, you had to know that you could not take on your captors when they clearly had the upper hand. Unless you knew that the political and military battles were going in your favor, you did not want to hassle them. You did not have to cooperate, but you also did not have to look for trouble. Most men realized that the best approach was to pull back and not be noticed. At times you even had to draw yourself into a protective cocoon, but there were also those moments when a man had to stand up for himself. The important thing was to pick your moments, and not push the envelop at the wrong time.

After the serious problems with food, shelter, and general care began to improve with the beginning of the truce talks in the summer of 1951, the biggest challenge was boredom. When a man is bored, he begins to feel sorry for himself, and he simply cannot allow himself to do so. This is not, however, the same as the so-called "the face-the-wall syndrome" in which the victim lost interest in everything, even life. He rolled on his side and refused to get out of bed or eat. These men were usually victims of pellagra, which is characterized by the 3 Ds: diarrhea, dermatitis, and dementia. The dementia caused apathy. They were often accused of "give-up-itis," but this was simply not true. These were terribly sick men, who, in the worst cases, had lost at least half of their body weight, no longer cared about anything, refused to eat or exercise, and simply turned their faces to the wall and died. They did not die because they gave up but because they suffered acute apathy caused by severe pellagra.

As a doctor, even without proper medicine, I could talk with those who still felt some hope and try to convince them that things were going to get better. Many of them just needed to be told that they were going to be all right. If you are a doctor, they will often listen to you.

◆   ◆   ◆

From the beginning, the Chinese tried to get us to collaborate, and you had to make up your mind you were not going to do it. Once the Chinese put pressure on a prisoner, and he gave in, he was at their mercy. There was an officer, whose name I won't mention, who was a very nice guy, but he had been pressured by the Chinese into collaborating. Once he did it the first time, the Chinese threatened to expose him to the rest of us if he did not continue to cooperate. Shortly before we were liberated, he finally stood up and said, "I have to confess to all of you. I have collaborated, and I am sorry." Evidently, he just could no longer do it. Everybody forgave him, because they understood the tremendous pressure the Chinese had put on him.

The one thing we could not forgive was ratting on a fellow prisoner. There was an essential difference between the Rats and most other collaborators. You might have some understanding why a man might cooperate under undue pressure, but doing so to get more cigarettes or to rat on a fellow prisoner was not acceptable. Most of the men were neither Progressives, Rats, nor even Reactionaries. They just tried to get by as best they could. I found that it was always the quiet, stalwart men who did their job well without complaining who best conducted themselves as prisoners. The loud-mouths were seldom helpful or supportive in camp.

With their long, tedious lectures, the Chinese political instructors were unrelenting in their attempts to break us down. After each lecture, we were asked to state or write our opinion. If anyone refused, he was labeled a Reactionary and punished. The Chinese might make him stand at attention in freezing weather with his shoes removed and holding a heavy limb overhead. If you lowered the limb, you were struck with a rifle butt. As a consequence, many men suffered frostbite and lost their toes or contracted pneumonia, and when no treatment was permitted, they died.

A man named Pritchett became a very outspoken anti-Communist who was always telling off the Chinese in Camp 5. Unfortunately, he did it one too many times. While he was serving time in the hole for attempting to escape, he was taken to camp headquarters, where the Chinese were celebrating May Day 1951 with lots of drinking and partying. The next day his dead body was returned to his squad room. I was called in to examine him. Pritchett had obviously been strangled. His face and tongue were blue, there were rope marks about his neck, and his face was bloated. I shouted at the Chinese officer who had accompanied the body that he had been strangled. He responded with a smile and said, "A rat crawled into his mouth and choked him."

The Chinese at times punished the wrong man. In the spring of 1951, several American POWs took food from a Chinese warehouse. The Chinese called out a man named Romero, who had nothing to do with it. They tied him up and beat him with sticks and a belt buckle until he "confessed." Those who had stolen the food felt guilty and eventually confessed, which embarrassed the Chinese.

The Chinese frequently used isolation holes for punishment. These were small, cave-like holes, maybe four feet square, which meant you could neither stand nor lie down, just sit or lean against the wall. Normally, there were no blankets and little food, and a political officer would come every day to remind you of the error in your thinking.

One hole I spent time in was dug into a little hillside, with pack mules tethered above, so their urine constantly oozed into the cell. The hole was damp and very cold. It had a barred, wooden gate in front with a guard outside, who was always nasty when his superiors were nearby. Typically, he'd hit you with his rifle butt when he pushed you into the hole, but if no one was around, he might be quite nice.

I recall one guard bringing me a cup of water after the political honcho left. He pointed to a small, carved crucifix I wore around my neck, first because I was Catholic and secondly to piss off the Communists who hated any religious symbols. He then opened his shirt to show me that he too was wearing a crucifix. He was a soldier because he had to be, so I could not be angry with him; in truth, I was never angry with the Korean or Chinese common people because I understood they were forced to live under a terrible and inhumane system.

Without anything to keep a man warm, the hole was especially bad in winter, although the summers could also be hot, humid, and miserable, especially during the monsoon season. It was very unpleasant when you had a nasty guard who refused to let you out to relieve yourself. At best, he might let you out once a day, but when that wasn't enough, you had to try and claw a hole in the ground and defecate into it. If you cooperated, they would feed you, but if you resisted, you might get nothing to eat or drink. Your treatment also reflected the pace of negotiations in P'anmunjom. When the truce talks were going badly, your treatment was worse and the meager food and water rations were cut back even more.

This punishment lasted either until you either wrote a confession to be read before your fellow POWs or further incarceration was thought to be of no use. We all realized that forced confessions meant nothing, and sometimes we were able to inject ridicule. For instance, a man might write, "I'm sorry I got caught speaking against communism" or "I'm sorry I called Comrade Wong a dirty, rotten son-of-a-bitch." Usually, the Communists were pleased with such confessions, and we got a good laugh out of them as well. But there were also men who never returned from their trip to the hole.

Drawing of a typical Punishment Hole in Camp 5

Later critics of American POW behavior in Korea argued that the British and the Turks supported each other better than we did, and sometimes they did. The key was they were mostly volunteer, career troops, who had lots of experience with each other in combat. It also helped that the Chinese did not have Turkish linguists to harangue them with their interminable lectures. The Turks did have a better survival record than we did, but the majority of them were captured after that first horrible winter, when the American survival rate also greatly improved.

After the negotiations began, and the Chinese begin providing more and better food and improved our living conditions, our death rate dropped almost to zero.

But the Turks were tough, and they had a discipline that would not have been permissible in our army. One Turk collaborated, and they damn near killed him. Their discipline was such that if you took away their commander, the next man would automatically step up and take over. This process worked all the way down until only two men were left, and one of them would then act as the leader. As a result, the Chinese pretty much left them alone. They had also been hardened over the centuries to live on a subsistence level that included food very similar to that which we were forced to eat in the camps. Over the generations, these marginal living conditions, along with the high death rates for children, undoubtedly weeded out the weaker strains of the population.

In late June 1951, a team of eleven male and female Chinese medical students arrived in Camp 5 accompanied by three times the medications of any earlier shipment. They may have meant well, but their training and medical skills were no better than their predecessors. One well-trained American corpsman could surpass these people in caring for the sick. Some of them, however, spoke a little English, so the Chinese cadre running the lower camp insisted I was no longer needed. I was discharged from all medical duties on July 19, 1951 and sent back to the officers' compound, where, like the rest of the officers, I was now supposed "to learn the truth."

As I've said so often, the Chinese could never be completely honest. As a result, they now had to invent some kind of excuse why they were moving me, and the reason, of course, had to be my fault. In truth, they could have simply said, "Take your bags and your butt up to the officers' compound," but they could not do that. Somehow, they had to make me responsible for the move.

A Chinese interpreter came to me and said, "Shadish, we need your forceps." I gave him the forceps. Within ten minutes he came trotting back with two armed guards and said, "We need your forceps." When I told him I had already given it to him, he said, "You lie. You sold it for your own profit. You are an evil man." They then threw me in the hole. Every day for two weeks they sent someone to the hole to ask what I had done with the forceps. The Chinese knew this was a lie, and they knew that I knew it was a lie, but they still had to carry out their charade.

Earlier in the month I had got in trouble with the Chinese over a pistol. I was holding sick call when all of a sudden there was a big commotion outside the dispensary. Two prisoners were on the ground fighting with each other, but it was actually a staged fight. The Chinese ran out of the building and left me in the sick room alone. A sergeant came running in and gave me a .45 pistol wrapped in a cloth. He told me to hide it in case someone might want to use it for an escape. I immediately shoved the gun underneath a bench, and that night I buried it underneath one of the stone steps outside the dispensary. When I was sent to the Officers' Compound a week later, I forgot all about the gun.

Several months later, a couple of Chinese guards with burp guns took me to Headquarters where Comrade Sund was very agitated. He screamed at me, "Where's the gun?" Sund, Dirty Picture Wong, and some others knocked me around a good bit. They kept threatening me, but I kept saying, "I don't what you're talking about. What gun?" I knew if they could prove I was involved with that gun, I would be in big trouble. So I continued to deny that I knew anything about it. Finally, I said, "Bring me the guy who says I have the gun, and I'll call him a liar to his face." Instead, they threw me in the hole again for several days. Each day a political honcho came by and asked me about the gun, but they finally turned me loose.

About the same time there was trouble over a camera. I was living in a room with prisoners the Chinese considered the most extreme reactionaries in the offic-ers' compound. The Chinese called our room "the Cage," because they consid-ered us to be no better than animals and wanted us separated from the other men. Walter Mayo, Clarence Anderson, and Johnny Thornton were my roommates, and we were always causing problems for the Chinese. I don't know how, but Mayo had somehow procured a small movie camera that he hid in a hole in the wall. We wanted to document the condition of an American named Ed Franklin, who had beriberi so bad that his scrotum swelled up to the size of a basketball. His legs were also so swollen they split and drained, which was common in such acute cases. We led Franklin out into the sunlight, where Anderson and I checked him out, while Mayo, hidden in the doorway, photographed the three of us with his camera.

A week or so later, Chinese guards burst into our room and shooed all of us out. They searched the room and found the camera, and threw Mayo in the hole. I know that no one from our room would ever have said anything, but somebody must have alerted them.

When I was transferred to the officers' compound, I was informed that neither I nor any other American or British physician was to practice any form of medi-cine, nor was I to "obstruct or undermine the work of the Chinese medical staff in the future." From this time forward I was in the same position as any other prisoner.

They told us their doctors would take care of us in the officers' compound, but, of course, they were incapable of doing so. In August 1951, they launched an immunization procedure using the surface scratch method. A Chinese doctor also injected a vaccine that was supposed to prevent typhoid, typhus, and cholera. Unfortunately, he used the same needle repeatedly with no sterilization between injections. After our prolonged insistence, he did wipe the needles with an alcohol solution between injections, but he still refused to boil the needles after each use. He also refused to excuse those who were ill from receiving the injection. A short time later we saw the beginning of an epidemic of infectious hepatitis, affecting some twenty men. Interestingly, this Chinese physician was never again seen in our compound, and when a few weeks later we received "booster" injections, sick men were excused and the needles were boiled before each injection.

Because I had devoted all my time to caring for the sick in the lower camp, I never had to attend the dreary indoctrination sessions. Occasionally, a Chinese cadre acting in the guise of a doctor had tried to discuss politics with me, but I was always allowed to defend my country without repercussions. This changed after I was sent to join the rest of the officers in their compound.

The lectures lasted from two to six hours every day but Sunday, and attendance was mandatory, even for the seriously ill, who had to leave their blankets on the wooden floors and sit for hours listening to the canned speeches of men we were ordered to call "Comrade" or "Instructor." These speeches covered economics, business, government, and religion. They were long, boring, and filled with lies, name-calling, and anti-American propaganda.

We were also supposed to discuss these lectures afterwards. After one typical diatribe on the evils of capitalism and the American way of life, Comrade Sund, whose tedious lectures were always the longest, looked at me and said, "Shadish, you will now discuss what I have talked about!"

I knew I was being baited so I refused to say anything except, "No comment."

He repeated his order, and when I continued my silence, I ended up in the hole for five days.

No dissent was allowed. Individual prisoners were often forced to stand and read articles from the New York or London *Daily Worker*, the San Francisco *People's World*, and the magazine *Masses and Main-Stream*. The lecture room contained a public address system, over which we received Peking Radio newscasts and editorials, along with a weird concoction of sounds called Chinese music.

None of this had any effect on the great majority of our men. You cannot ram nonsense down the throat of the average American. Predictably, we hated every minute of these programs and did everything in our power to resist them. Yet, these sessions lasted without interruption until we officers left Camp 5 in October 1951, and we were to get more of the same in Camp 2.

There were many widely admired men in Camp 5, but without a doubt Father Emil Kapaun, who was a Catholic chaplain, topped the list. He is presently being reviewed for sainthood, and I certainly believe he is deserving. I knew him only briefly and at a distance. There was a small strip of land that separated the officers' and the enlisted men's compounds that was off limits to all of us in Camp 5. Nevertheless, Father Kapaun would stroll over this forbidden piece of land looking for any kind of vegetation that might be edible. For some reason, he was not harassed by the Chinese. I think they were in awe and maybe even a little afraid of him. One morning, as I sat on my clinic step awaiting sick call, a man approached and shouted, "Hello Doctor. I'm Father Kapaun." I yelled back, "Hello Father." He then shouted, "God bless you, Doctor," and returned to the officers' compound. He would periodically walk by and always repeat his greeting. I hope he knew what a boost his words were. I later learned much more about this wonderful man. Although he had a leg wound, he ignored his own difficulties while helping everyone else in myriad ways. He would even steal food for the men from the Chinese, after saying something like, "Father forgive me." Eventually, the infection in his leg became so bad that the Chinese took him to the hospital but permitted no treatment. He died there on May 23, 1951, after trying to cheer up his fellow prisoners to the very end. When he saw them crying because he was terminally ill, he said, "Don't cry for me. I'm going to a better place." He was not only a priest but a genuine and caring human being.

Captain Jerry Fink was a Marine pilot and another outstanding individual. When Jerry first came into camp he was a big, husky guy who pulled no punches. When the Chinese asked him why he was in Korea, he said, "I'm here to kill all you goddam Chinese." But Jerry had a very big heart and was a very talented wood carver. Although he was Jewish, he carved a crucifix for Father Kapaun, and he also carved a stethoscope for me. He got a piece of wood and used a nail to drill a hole through it, and tapered up on both ends. It worked very well.

Alexander Boysen (left) shows a scalpel fashioned from a boot's steel reinforcement rod. William Shadish holds the wooden stethoscope carved for him by Jerry Fink. This photo was taken in Tokyo General Army Hospital shortly after liberation.

IN MEMORY
OF
FATHER
EMIL J. KAPAUN
DIED IN
COMMUNIST
PRISONER OF WAR
CAMP
MAY 23 1951

LORD IT IS TRUE
THY YOKE IS EASY
THY BURDEN LIGHT
I HAVE OFTEN
EXPERIENCED THAT
IT IS PLEASANT
AND COMFORTING TO
BEAR THE BURDEN
OF DUTY
I WOULD RATHER DIE
FOR THE TRUE VALUES
OF LIFE THAN LIVE
FOR THE FALSE
100 DAYS INDULGENCE
GRANTED BY
THE MOST REV JAMES A. McNULTY
BISHOP OF PATERSON

Jerry Fink transported his carved tribute to Father Kapaun back to the States after liberation. It now hangs in Father Kapaun High School in Wichita, Kansas.

Johnny Thornton was another unforgettable man. We called him "Rotorhead" because he had been a navy helicopter pilot. He was short, stocky, bald, and he always kept us laughing. He was also always in trouble with the Chinese, and sometimes we got into trouble together. One day when the Chinese were harassing him in Camp 5, he referred to them as "You fucking Chinese." They hauled him off to the punishment hole. When he finally came back to the room, everyone, of course, asked, "What happened to you?" When he told us, we all started laughing. Someone asked, "What do you think about Johnny's comment, Doc?"

I said, "You mean to tell me the Chinese don't know about fucking when there are 300,000,000 of them?" Bang! The door flew open. Comrade Sund, who was constantly on my case, had been listening to us. He ordered me to go with him, and it was back to the hole for another week.

I have already mentioned that anytime you did something the Chinese considered wrong, you had to write a confession, and then read it aloud to your colleagues. When I wrote my confession this time, I wrote, "I don't understand why the fucking Chinese were upset that we called them 'fucking Chinese'." And I just kept repeating the same thing. Finally, I wrote, "I'm sorry I got caught saying 'fucking Chinese'." They accepted that.

Shortly after this incident, Johnny and I got in trouble again, this time over a chicken. We were walking along the barbed-wire fence that surrounded the Chinese compound, and we spotted a bunch of chickens that were meant exclusively for the Chinese officers. We were starving and Johnny opined how he would love to have some chicken, and I had to agree with him. The next morning before daylight Johnny crawled through the fence, grabbed one of the chickens, broke its neck so it wouldn't squawk, and carried it back through the fence. We plucked and gutted it and threw the feathers and guts down an old, dry well in the middle of our compound. We then took it back to the Cage. Our rooms were heated by tunnels underneath the floors. After building a fire at one end, the heat and smoke went through these tunnels and came out the other end. We knew if we put the chicken in the opening, the Chinese would be able to tell there was a fire. We also had no wood. The day before Comrade Sund had lectured us on how we should respect the people's property and not damage it, so we decided to knock a hole through the floor and into the tunnel below. We then went to the Chinese and told them there was a hole in our heating tunnel but that we wanted to fix the people's property. They thought that was great. We got some mud and made a putty-like substance and patched the hole and repaired the floor. Next we told them we had to dry it, but that we didn't have any wood. They were so happy we were doing the people's work that they gave us wood, and we started a fire. We cut up the chicken and put the pieces on long sticks and stuck them up in the flues. Our mouths began watering, but just then we were called out for a lecture session on the hill overlooking our room. We were sitting there listening to all this crap about evil Wall Street war mongers and their exploitation of the poor, when, all of a sudden, we began to smell the odor of cooking chicken. Comrade Sund began sniffing and quickly dismissed us and began searching for the source. Sure enough, there were those roasting pieces of chicken stuck up in the flues of the Cage. Sund lined us up and asked each of us, "You like chickee?"

We all answered, "Oh, we love chickee. Are you going to give us some chickee?"

Sund angrily responded, "No! Did you do this?"

We said, "No, we did not do this."

Sund said, "But there's chickee in your fire."

We told him, "You just lectured us on the exploitation of the workers. Someone in this camp, and we certainly don't know who, has exploited the work we performed for the people when we repaired our heating tunnel."

The fact that we used parts of his lecture truly dumbfounded him, and he had to let us go. From then on, including at our reunions over the past fifty years, the former members of the Cage always greet each other with, "You like chickee?"

As the negotiations dragged on, the Chinese began to realize they were going to have to answer to the rest of the world why so many prisoners had died under their care. Back when I was still treating the enlisted men, the Chinese had ordered me to stop the dying. I told them that the only way I could do that was if they gave us sufficient food and medicine. Then, after I was moved to the officers' compound, I was ordered to sign a statement that all deceased American prisoners had died of syphilis they had contracted before leaving the United States. I told them I could never sign such a statement. They told me that unless I did, I would never go home. I had to tell them, "Do whatever you want with me, because if I sign such a statement, there is no way I could ever go home." I was actually ready to die rather than sign that kind of lie, and I never did, although they tried several times to make me do so.

The Communists simply could never be truthful, and because of this we have to understand we can never negotiate with them, even today, because the North Koreans and the Chinese will never tell the truth. As long as they are Communists, they will violate any agreement they enter. Clearly, they figured that if you tell a lie often enough, some people will believe it. As much as anything else about my incarceration, it was this Communist need to lie that has stuck with me.

This was reenforced later when I saw a vaguely familiar Chinese officer walk into Camp 2, replete with epaulettes and high boots. Soon the guards came in and took me into a room where this officer was sitting at a table loaded with good food. He asked, "Do you remember me?" I told him I did not. He said, "My name is Kuo Tsien-tsu, and you saved my life in Hofong." He was the officer I had given the sulfadiazine tablets back in Death Valley. He said, "I want you to eat with me and we'll talk."

I told him, "As long as you do not ask me to make any political statements, I will talk with you."

He said, "No, just the two of us will talk." The first thing he asked me was why I had saved his life. I told him, "I'm a physician and I took an oath to try to help anyone who is sick. If I saw you on the battlefield, I would shoot you, but you asked for my help so I helped you."

He said, "That's what's wrong with your people. They teach you how to cure, not who to cure."

Then I said to him, "Look out that window. Those are my men walking around. You are trying to teach us to be Communists. Do you understand that the poorest man out there will live better than you will ever experience in your life? So, how can you convince us to be Communists?"

He held up his finger and thumb about a quarter of an inch apart and said, "If we can sow this much doubt in your mind and that of your men, we win."

He was right. If you can make men begin to doubt their way of life, you have a tremendous advantage in exerting control over them, but the fact the Communists were not successful in doing so, except in a few isolated cases, was a great tribute to our men and the American way of life.

7

CAMP TWO—PIN-CHONG-NI

○ ○
Get a match stick and scratch it.

—Chinese doctor's prescription
for inflammation of the ear canal

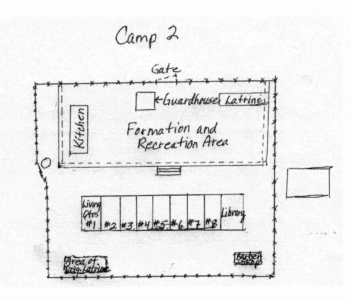

The lower compound of Camp 2

On October 21, 1951, all the officers from the upper compound of Camp 5, in addition to several Air Force NCOs, were marched seven or eight miles to Camp

2, which was located in the village of Pin-Chong-Ni. We were to remain there for twenty-two long months until we were finally liberated in early September 1953.

The Chinese informed us that they were assembling the officers from all POW camps in Camp 2, and within a month our numbers swelled to between 300 and 350 men. There was a small area for the senior grade officers, and the rest of us were put in a lower compound that was a couple of acres in size and surrounded by a barbed wire fence. By splitting us up, I'm sure the Chinese were again hoping to implement their divide and conquer strategy.

Our compound consisted of a cookhouse, a latrine, and a schoolhouse that was built by the Japanese during its occupation of Korea. There were several six—or seven-inch stone steps leading up to the schoolhouse, but when I tried to climb them, I discovered I was so weak from our miserably inadequate diet that I could not raise my leg high enough to climb a single step. I had to put my hands around my thigh and lift my leg. I was shocked to discover that my hands passed completely around my thigh and met on the other side. I had weighed 200 pounds when I arrived in Korea, with full, muscular thighs. Not anymore!

We were divided into eight squads of twenty-four men each, and each squad was assigned to a room in the schoolhouse, which was infested with rats, flies, mosquitoes, and cockroaches. The schoolhouse also contained an assembly room which doubled as a library containing various Communist publications and a lecture hall for the indoctrination sessions.

We slept on the floor twelve men to a side perpendicular to a central walkway that went down the center of the room. In April of 1953, during the final negotiations for Operation Little Switch, the Chinese finally gave us material to build double-decker bunk beds, but we never received mattresses. The rooms were drafty and very cold despite each room having a smoky, tin-barrel stove. We received a 300-pound weekly ration of wood, but that was never enough in winter.

Those of us who were considered reactionaries were assigned to Squad Room #1, and I lucked out in my immediate sleeping companions. On one side was Lt. Bill Whiteside and on the other was Lt. Denis Earp, who was a South African pilot. Bill was cheerful and uplifting. He had sung professionally, and he touched us deeply with his renditions of songs like *Going Home* and *The Prisoner's Song*. Denis, who later became the Commanding General of the South African Air Force, was remarkable, charming, and full of knowledge and pride of South Africa. He taught us the Zulu War Chant and the stomp that accompanied it. Other members of Squad Room #1 included Clarence Anderson, Joe Manto, Michael Lorenzo, and my old buddy, Johnny Thornton.

Anderson, Alexander M. Boysen, Sidney Esensten, and Gene Lam were the other American doctors in Camp 2, and we all made it home.[1] Anderson was the senior doctor and a very good man. He had run the hospital in Camp 5, which was a death house where the men went to die; Esensten worked with Clarence Anderson; Boysen, who had been on the infamous Tiger Death March, was tall, thin, blonde-haired, quiet, and very reliable; Gene N. Lam was also very quiet and dependable and a wonderful person who had been with me in Death Valley. In fact, he saved my life in Death Valley when I became critically ill with dysentery. We all suffered from chronic diarrhea, but if you also had a fever, you had dysentery, and I had a high fever. I had to run out to the slit trench ten to fifteen times a day. While returning from one of these trips, I fell down and could not get up. I called out for somebody to come and help me. Gene Lam came and pulled me back to the shed. He later told me I was unconscious by this time. He fed me and got hot water and some sulfa tablets for me. I have no idea how long I was out, but he stayed and took care of me.

There were also three British doctors in Camp 2: Sandy Ferrie, Bob Hickey, and Doug Patchett. The Chinese, however, allowed none of us to practice medicine. They told us we were not needed because they had their own doctors. They said the same thing when we asked them about Red Cross packages: "You don't need them because we take care of you." But, of course, they did not.

The first Chinese physician we encountered in Camp 2 was both incompetent and uncooperative. He was replaced in late 1952 by a Dr. Tang, who claimed to have studied and performed a resident surgeon's duties at Peking Union Medical College for five years. He was better than any other Chinese physician I encountered, but his knowledge was also limited.

We had sporadic dental care. The Chinese had one kit of dental equipment, consisting of four varieties of forceps, all made in Czechoslovakia. However, this kit rotated among all the prison camps. We had it four times in the entire twenty months I was in Camp 2, and each time for only two or three days. The first time we had the kit the Chinese physician was determined to perform all the extractions, but when he ran into complications he could not handle, he called me in. The second time, Bob Hickey and I were allowed to perform the extractions. The next time I performed all the extractions myself because Hickey had been moved to another part of the camp. We had 2-4cc of 2 percent procaine per procedure, a

---

1. As mentioned in Chapter 5, American physicians Edwin Ecklund died in Death Valley and Burt Coers and Peter Kubinek in Camp 5. There was another American doctor named Gravelin who died after he was captured, but Shadish never saw or met him.

10cc syringe, and one and a quarter-inch, 24-gauge needle. We had a small steril-izing tray and a bottle of iodine tincture.

Just before repatriation, a Chinese dentist visited Camp 2 for a couple of days and did several extractions and a number of fillings made of a putty-like material. The only preparation for this was a crude scraping of the decayed area with a small instrument. All these fillings fell out within one-half hour to ten days after insertion.

The majority of the men who had extractions done by the Chinese also devel-oped an infection of the sockets. Most of those we did healed nicely without infection. I attribute this difference to the fact that the Chinese were both impet-uous and rough, and did not bother to clean up the sockets after extractions. Consequently, most of their cases had alveolar wall fracture to a degree that must be considered avoidable. When this debris was not removed, it led to prolonged drainage and slow healing.

Two Chinese "specialists" visited camp shortly before the armistice. One was an ophthalmologist and the other an otolaryngologist. A measure of their incom-petence occurred when a prisoner who had chronic external otitis, which is an inflammation of the ear canal, asked the otolaryngologist what he should do if the itching persisted. The "specialist" told him, "Get a matchstick and scratch it."

◆   ◆   ◆

The first truce talks were held in Kaesong on July 10, 1951. They were later moved to P'anmunjom, where on November 27, 1951 the two sides agreed on the first cease-fire line. Shortly thereafter they also exchanged lists of prisoners. Unfortunately, the more than 100 additional plenary sessions over the next twenty months made it clear the war was as much about ideology and propa-ganda as it was about battlefield victories. The major sticking point was repatria-tion. The Communists insisted that all prisoners held by the UN forces had to be returned to their native country, but tens of thousands of these prisoners refused to do so, which, of course, was a terrible embarrassment for China and North Korea.

The exchange of prisoner names was all important. Before this exchange, the United States government had little if any information concerning who had been captured and who was still alive in the camps. Now, with the entire world watch-ing, the Chinese and North Koreans would have to account for those prisoners who were still alive. I already mentioned how the Chinese tried to make me sign a statement that the cause of death for every American who had died at their hands was due to syphilis contracted before coming to Korea. Now they had to obscure how malnourished and debilitated their prisoners had become under their so-called lenient care. As a result, our food began to improve to a life-sustaining level, and our death rates dropped abruptly to almost zero. Rice became a daily staple, and we got some vegetables and occasionally a little meat. Our diet became almost sufficient in caloric value, although still deficient in just about everything else.

Our kitchen crew, which was now excused from all other details, would get up early and boil water in large pots to make it safe for drinking and cooking. Our cooks were very ingenious. They would allow the bottom layer of rice to burn and then scrap it up and make something that tasted a little like coffee. We had lots of sorghum, which is a purplish grain that we feed to pigs in America. Small loaves of bread could be made from it, but sorghum is very deficient in Vitamin B-5, without which one is susceptible to pellagra.

For Christmas and Thanksgiving, if all was going well with the negotiations, we received eggs, cigarettes, candy, tea, and even a pig that was supposed to feed more than 300 men. It would be butchered and cut up so everyone would get a small bowl of soup with a tiny cube of pork in it. We received two issues of clothing per year in Camp 2, which consisted of one summer and one winter uniform. The summer issue included two thin blue cotton shirts, two pairs of trousers, one white undershirt and shorts, and a pair of tennis shoes. The winter uniform was made of blue padded cotton and included a jacket, a hat, one pair of trousers, a cotton undershirt and shorts, and one pair of padded tennis shoes. Socks were issued less often. We also each received a blanket and a padded overcoat.

When allowed, we worked hard on improving conditions in Camp 2. Shortly after arriving, our own senior officers assigned me to be the Camp Sanitation Officer. My duties included inspections of the kitchen, latrine, living quarters, and recreational areas. The large hill behind the schoolhouse constituted a large watershed. To combat the constant drainage problems this caused during the rainy season, we dug large ditches around the area. I also was able to have the latrine moved as far as possible from the kitchen. I then requested a washroom, which eventually was approved. We converted one large room near the kitchen into a bathhouse, with a large eight-foot square tub with two-foot sides. We heated water in the kitchen and an entire squad could bathe at the same time. It was heaven to be able to wash in warm water. The Chinese gave us toothbrushes and soap, which we used both for washing and for toothpaste. In the spring of 1952, they also gave us two sets of barbering tools, and we converted a small room in the back of the schoolhouse into a barbershop.

We finally began receiving mail on a semi-regular basis, which was very heartening. Our families did not officially know that we were POWs until near the end of 1951, and in some cases early 1952, and we rarely received any mail before early 1952. My family had a good idea I was alive because they saw a photograph the Chinese sent to many of our hometown newspapers for propaganda purposes, but they received no mail from me for fourteen months. I have a collection of envelops that have no postmarks on them but were stamped by the International Red Cross. These were the first communications that were sent, perhaps through the Chinese Red Cross, to our families, but they all arrived empty. I have never been able to find out what was in them. After that, our letters began arriving irregularly.

Some men received a lot of mail, and some received only one or two letters during their entire time in captivity. The Chinese did threaten to withhold our mail by saying, "If you do not cooperate, we will not give you any mail," but I am not sure they followed through on this. I seldom cooperated, and I received probably a dozen or more letters in my three years, which I think was about average. It also did not seem to matter whether you were a Reactionary or a Progressive. Some Reactionaries received a lot of mail, but others got none, and the same thing happened with the Progressives. I have no idea why this was the case.

The Chinese denied censoring our mail, but they certainly did. For example, my wife usually included photographs of the children and her in her letters. In one letter, however, the photograph was of some other woman and children, although "To Bill" was written on the back. I was trying to figure out who they were when Lieutenant Billy Foshee walked by asking, "Does anyone have a letter with the wrong photographs in it?" After opening our mail the Chinese had clearly put the photos back in the wrong envelop.

I also remember a Chinese interpreter coming up to me, after obviously opening my mail, and saying, "The government had your wife and children pose with a new car in Washington to propagandize how good life is in America."

I told him, "No, we own that car."

But he insisted, "You could not own that car." He really believed that no common person could own his own automobile.

When you wrote a letter, you did not dare say anything bad about the Chinese or the conditions in the camp. If you did, the letter would never be sent. You had to disguise what you wanted to say. For example, in one of my letters I wrote, "We are being treated well, and they are giving us food, but the only food I really miss is Red Heart." Red Heart was dog food, and my family immediately understood that I really meant I would eat dog food if I could get it. A lot of guys wrote things between the lines to get the message out, but most of the time we simply wrote we were doing all right because we did not want our families to worry any more about us than they already were.

The Chinese also tried to propagandize our letters, but we wouldn't stand for this. For example, we found out that they were stamping a return address on our letters that stated, "The Chinese Volunteers for Peace and Against American Aggression." When we discovered this, we all refused to write any more letters. We won this battle, and they eliminated "against American aggression."

The mail, like everything else, was affected by the state of the continuing peace talks. If negotiations were going well, the Chinese would give us our letters, but when the talks broke down, they stopped our mail, decreased our rations, and increased their lectures and the general harshness of our treatment. Nevertheless, with conditions generally improving, our physical and mental health improved, and we were more inclined to try and get the better of the Chinese.

One of the most fun things we did to torment the Chinese was to launch what we called Crazy Week. Johnny Thornton kicked off Crazy Week with his imaginary motorcycle.[2] He would mount his "motorcycle," yell, "Zoom! Zoom! Zoom!" and motor around the camp. The Chinese watched him and were clearly puzzled. I think they suspected he might be a little off in the head. The Chinese become very nervous around people they consider to be insane. They asked me, "Shadish, what's wrong with him?"

I tapped my head and replied, "He's crazy."

That clearly worried them, and they continued watching him. Finally, they could no longer stand it, and Commander Ding, whom we called "The Snake" because he was very tall man with weird, beady eyes, called us out and gave us one of his long lectures. Typically, he would talk for five minutes, and the interpreter would say, "Commander Ding says hello." But this time he ordered Thornton to stop and take his place in formation. Thornton zoomed up on his imaginary motorcycle and Commander Ding said, "You know, Thornton, that in Communism nobody can have what everyone cannot have. Others in the camp cannot have a motorcycle, so you have to give up yours."

Johnny started crying, "Please, don't take my motorcycle." He really put on a show.

But Commander Ding said again, "Yes, you have to give up your motorcycle."

---

2.   Helicopter pilot Captain John W. Thornton told his story in *Believed to Be Alive* (Annapolis: Naval Institute Press), 1981.

Johnny finally said, "Okay," and he handed it over to one of the Chinese guards who went zoom, zoom, zoom and took it away. Of course, the rest of us were howling by this time.

Even after the end of Crazy Week Johnny kept doing outrageous things. There was a political cadre we called "Tilt" because when he got upset he bounced around just like a pin ball machine. He had given us some seeds to grow daikons, which is like a big white radish, so we would have our own vegetables. But when the daikon matured, Tilt harvested it for his own use. This really upset Johnny so he sneaked into the garden, cut the tops off all the daikons, took the root of the plant, and then put the tops back over the empty holes. The next morning, when Tilt came to pick his daikon, just the tops came off. Tilt became so agitated that he suffered a nervous breakdown and had to be led away by two guards.

We also had a particularly nasty guard in Camp 2 who would wake us up between 4:30 and 5 o'clock to fall out for roll call. He would come into our squad room and start kicking our feet and yelling, "Get up! Get up!" We finally decided we had to do something. This one morning we all got up well before he arrived and got dressed. When he opened the door and started hollering at us to get up, we just ran over him. When he recovered and followed us out the door, he was really angry, but the commander was already congratulating us for falling out so early, so he couldn't say a word.

If we ever left anything in the aisle, this same ugly guard would kick it. So Johnny filled his shoe with small rocks and set it on the floor. When the guard kicked it with his soft tennis shoe, he almost broke his toe, and we all howled in delight.

We also tormented a guard we called "Dirty Picture Wong." He got his name when two of our guys, thinking he was out of his room, sneaked in hoping to find food and anything else that might prove useful. What they found was Dirty Picture Wong looking at some pictures in a girlie magazine and masturbating. This was certainly not acceptable Communist behavior, so Wong could not report them for breaking into his room, nor did he bother any of us after this incident.

By this time the Chinese seemed to sense that their iron grip on us was slipping. We were occasionally assembled in the exercise yard for surprise inspections, usually in the middle of the night or very early in the morning, and these too became a chance to exhibit our resistance. For one such inspection, we were ordered to strip to our shorts and stand outside while our rooms, clothing, and belongings were searched for contraband. The Chinese were so puritanical that we were not required to remove our undershorts. The political commissar approached each man and asked about hidden weapons and all kinds of things. When he approached Captain Ralph Nardella, Ralph employed a maneuver he had practiced for just such a moment. Ralph had developed gyneomastia, which meant his breasts had become enlarged because of malnutrition. By alternately tensing his neck muscles, he could significantly twitch his breasts. When Ralph proceeded to do so, the commissar ordered him to stop, but Ralph pleaded that he was so cold he could not control his irritated muscles. When he continued to twitch his breasts, the Chinese officer gave him his clothes and dismissed him.

Ralph always kept us laughing. Comrade "Chickee-Chickee" Sund was an irritating bastard, always looking for reasons to punish us, while at the same time trying to befriend us. His English, however, was not very good. Realizing this, Ralph would walk up to him, put his arm around his shoulders, and say, "Sund, you great big son-of-a-bitch, how are you?" Sund would brighten and mumble some nicety. I don't think he ever realized what the phrase meant.

Doing things like this really helped our mental state, and although the Chinese might retaliate, we knew they were no longer going to kill us. One day the Chinese announced, "Beginning tomorrow, the squad leaders must report and salute the enlisted man who will be taking attendance and reporting any men who have escaped." Then, they appointed new squad leaders, including making me leader of Squad One.

Once again, I knew I was being set up, so I told my guys, "Bullshit, we are not going to do this." Our senior Army officer wasn't worth a damn. He was simply too afraid to do anything, so I went to the senior Marine officer, Major John McLaughlin, a man who ended up a major general and whom I respected more than anyone else in camp. I said to him, "Mac, if I refuse to salute and report escapees, there will be trouble for the entire camp. However, I also believe that the Chinese are losing control, and I think we can better ourselves if we refuse to cooperate. I want to tell them we won't do it."

Major McLaughlin asked, "Are you willing to do this? You know you'll be put in the hole."

I told him, "Sure, because I don't think they can kill us now." He then told me to go ahead and refuse to salute.

The next morning, when the Chinese officer told me to report, I said no. They immediately took me away to the hole. Next, a Captain Milford Stanley, a black officer, was put in the punishment hole next to mine and so on all the way down the line. Every squad leader after me said no. The Chinese were really upset. They were afraid they were losing control so they had to pressure us to recant. We were visited daily by political honchos who harangued and threatened us if we did not confess, repent, and return to the camp. For six days, we all refused. On the seventh day, the Chinese brought in an American major who had already been severely tortured. He had gone through hell trying not to tell them anything, but they had broken him. He said to us, "Look guys, our senior officer has asked me to tell you to go ahead and report the way the Chinese want you to. You need to sign this paper that you will do this." We argued, but he insisted this was an order from our senior officer. We did sign because we thought we had been ordered to do so; however, when we got back to the camp, we discovered that the senior officer had done no such thing. The major had been forced to lie about this, but he had been tortured so severely we did not hold it against him. After the war I testified before an Army Intelligence (G2) investigating committee that he had been tortured so extensively that he "was incapable mentally of offering resistance."[3] Interestingly, the Chinese order to report and salute was never issued again, and we were all happily relieved of our positions as squad leaders. I honestly believed we could have held out and won this confrontation, and maybe we did.

How far to carry one's resistance is a difficult decision. In one of our earlier indoctrination sessions, the Chinese gave Major Hume a copy of some propaganda material condemning the U. S. and asked what he thought of it. He told them, "It's not worth the paper it's printed on." For this he was put in the punishment hole and kept there until he died. His punishment was for "insulting the people's paper."

The indoctrination sessions gradually decreased in number and length until they stopped altogether in March 1952. By then, the Chinese had possibly recognized the futility of their lectures, but more likely they feared increasingly negative international exposure. Chinese newspapers had begun reporting that the United States was falsely accusing China of forcing POWs to study Communism, and they did not want to be caught in another lie. Whatever the reason, the Chinese now began encouraging us to entertain ourselves. They gave us equipment for playing softball and soccer, as well as playing cards and chess boards. I organized the American soccer team and we played against the British and the Turkish teams. We did very well against the British, but not so well against the Turks.

---

3.   "Summary of Information," Office of the Assistant Chief of Staff, G2, Military District of Washington, Dossier No. C8054479. Sent to Dr. Shadish under the 1992 Freedom of Information Act.

Captain Kazam was a Turkish friend who played fullback on his seven-man team. I played center forward on the American team. During our final game we were tied, and Bill Whiteside made a beautiful pass just ahead of me about twenty-five yards in front of the Turkish goal. Both Kazam and I rushed for the ball. Seeing him coming up fast, I swung my leg in a real haymaker. Unfortunately, I did not beat him to the ball. I can still remember the smile on his face when my foot struck the ball immobilized against his foot. My foot bounced back with a crack. I had dislocated my big toe. Dr. Anderson manipulated the toe back into its proper place, and to this day that toe remains stiff.

Hoping for wide distribution, the Chinese put together this propaganda brochure, featuring photos and stories of the Inter-Camp Olympics.

Between November 15–27, 1952, the Chinese organized the Inter-Camp Olympics, obviously for propaganda purposes. They held the Games just outside of Camp 5 in Pyŏktong, and invited participants from all of the camps. Recognizing the political nature of the Games, some men refused to participate, including my soccer team, but others thought going would give them a chance to talk to prisoners, especially the enlisted men from other camps, in addition to being a welcome diversion.

In late 1952, the Chinese launched their "Germ Warfare" propaganda campaign, and, as usual, they hid the truth. Due to poor food, a lack of sanitation, and inadequate health care, there had been a severe outbreak of smallpox among the Chinese and North Korean troops and civilians. Shortly after liberation, when I met General Crawford Sams in New York, he told me about parachuting into North Korean controlled territory at night with South Korean commandos and visiting a North Korean hospital ward. Using a flashlight, Sams discovered that the patients were suffering from smallpox.

We were confident that there was nothing to the Chinese accusations of germ warfare, especially after they put up all kinds of phony pictures in this small building. Then, after one of our bombers dropped anti-radar tinsel, the Chinese really went crazy. They put on white uniforms and gloves, pointed at the tinsel, and screamed, "Germ Warfare!" One of our Air Force officers, recognizing what the material actually was, picked up several pieces, and stuffed them in his mouth. The Chinese were shocked. An officer named Bob Wright found a dead mouse, made a tiny parachute out of a piece of cloth and some string, and hung it from a tree. The Chinese had no idea how to handle behavior like this.

Several American pilots were shot down during this "Germ Warfare" flap and brought into our camp, but they were kept segregated from us in nearby huts. We could see them when we went on our wood runs but were not allowed any contact. The Chinese were determined to make the world think we were guilty of germ warfare so they put tremendous pressure on these men to "confess," and some were successfully coerced into doing so. Those guys had it very rough, and I would guess that some of them died during those interrogations.

During the latter part of 1952, our senior officers made a considerable effort to secretly organize resistance efforts in the camps. Apparently the Chinese got wind of this and a number of these officers were put into solitary confinement for several months.

In spite of the germ warfare controversy and the agonizingly slow pace of negotiations, conditions continued gradually to improve. We were even able to worship the way we pleased. Padre Sam Davies was an Anglican clergyman and chaplain who was small in stature but big in heart. He steadfastly and openly practiced Christianity despite being harassed and punished by the Chinese Communists, who required him to submit his sermons in advance, after which he was criticized and forced to change the content. At one point, he was punished and put in solitary confinement outside the camp. When this happened, we lined up at the fence facing where he was confined and loudly sang, "Faith of our Fathers." This was his favorite hymn, and he had often led us in its singing. But now things had changed, and he was allowed to hold services without much interference. The rest of us took this to heart and became more and more convinced that we would soon be liberated.

8

GOING HOME!

o o o o o o o o o o o o o o o o o o o o o o o o o o o o o o o o o o o

We few, we happy few, we band of brothers.

—*William Shakespeare, King Henry V*

After we were captured, I tried to tell the guys we were going to be prisoners for a long time, but from the very beginning there were always rumors circulating through camp that we would soon be going home. Several times I bet on the cuff that the war would not be over within a year, and for a long time I won.

Our best source of news was from recently captured prisoners. We also looked for information in the *Shanghai News* and the *London Daily Worker*, but we were always disappointed. Both printed nothing but propaganda stories about warmongering capitalists and all the glorious victories the Communists were winning on the battlefield, but we knew from recently downed airmen that this was untrue. There was nothing in these newspapers about the unresolved repatriation issue that made the war drag on for an extra twenty months. The Chinese could not admit that tens of thousands of their soldiers who were being held captive in South Korea did not want to return to North Korea or China.[1] Instead, they would tell us, "We have agreed to everything, but the Americans do not want the war to end." I did not hear anything about the revolt the North Korean and Chinese prisoners staged on Koje-do Island, but I know exactly what the Communists would have written: "Our men are being tortured and killed and therefore

---

1.   An April 1952 United Nations screening of the 132,000 military and civilian North Korean and Chinese internees determined that less than half wanted to return to their homeland. For an interesting discussion of the prisoner repatriation issue, see T. R. Fehrenbach, *This Kind of War: A Study in Unpreparedness* (New York: Macmillan, 1963), 383, 415, 440, 450.

they had to fight back to save their lives from the vicious warmongering capital-ists."

The first sizeable numbers of UN prisoners were liberated between April 20–26, 1953 as part of Operation Little Switch; however, once again Chinese duplic-ity marred what was supposed to be an exchange of sick and wounded prisoners. The plan was for 471 South Koreans, 149 Americans, and 64 from other UN nations to be exchanged for 5,800 Communist prisoners. In preparation for this switch, the Chinese asked those of us who had practiced medicine to put together a list of prisoners whose physical problems made them obvious choices for early repatriation. The Chinese did select a few names from our list but ignored most of them, preferring to send home those men they considered to be Progressives. Not everyone sent home in Little Switch was a Progressive, but all the Progres-sives the Chinese wanted to send back to the States were included. This infuri-ated us and we argued vehemently, but the Chinese insisted their doctors knew better than we did who the really sick and wounded were.

So once again, the Chinese had lied to the rest of the world. For example, Tom Harrison was an officer in our camp who had lost a leg and should certainly have been sent home but was not. There were also many others with crippling injuries or chronic illnesses who were not included. The Chinese were hoping that these Progressives would spread the communist ideology after their return to the States, but they made a big mistake. Most of these men were not doctrinaire or committed Progressives. They tended to be individuals who went along with the party line in order to survive. A lot of them had set out to resist the Chinese and their Communist propaganda, but when they were pushed, they signed peti-tions or statements for what they considered their own self-protection.

Such men were certainly not going home to try and start a revolution.[2] It is just common sense that someone who is willing to compromise his character and principles in his own self-interest will do so wherever he is or whatever the situa-

---

2. According to Raymond Lech, at least 20 percent of the returning Progressives "remained active in the movement for which they had studied for three long, hard years.... By October 1953 hundreds of soldiers and former soldiers were back in the United States with 'missions' inspired and controlled by the Peking government." Although the Chinese certainly hoped their indoctrination programs would bear fruit in the U.S., this sounds more like the plot of *The Manchurian Candidate* than it does reality. Lech offers no evidence for his conclusion that such missions were "frighteningly successful," and no other historians of the period mention such activ-ities. See Raymond B. Lech, *Broken Soldiers* (Urbana: University of Illinois Press, 2000), 185, 193-194.

tion. I also believe that these men realized what they had at home was vastly superior to anything the Communists had to offer.

Unfortunately, the men in Operation Little Switch were sent home on a slow ship, which gave army psychiatrist Dr. William Mayer lots of time to interrogate them. When he discovered that a few of them had collaborated, he asked them how many of the others had also cooperated with their captors. To protect themselves, they told him that everyone had. Mayer took this as gospel truth and built it into a dishonest and distorted crusade against all Korean War prisoners, which marked the beginning of many years of vilification of good and loyal American soldiers.

In the four months between Operation Little Switch and our final liberation, the Chinese wanted to show the world how well they had treated us, so they began to give us lots of good food. Having been without proper nutrition for so long, we naturally ate all we could. We did not gain back all the weight we had lost, but when we crossed the line to freedom, we certainly looked nothing like the human skeletons we had been earlier in our captivity. The Chinese also stopped harassing us, gave us more recreational equipment, and even tried to mingle and talk with us.

With things going so much better, we knew that the rest of us would soon be going home, but we did not know precisely when. Then, one evening something very unique happened in the heavens. The weather in Korea varied but it was always extreme: dry, hot summers, cold, cold winters, with monsoon rains mixed in between. It was July 27, 1953, and I was sitting in front of our building watching the sun go down. The sun was blood red, and I had never seen anything quite like it. I said to a buddy, "Look at that. Something must be going on." Sure enough, both sides had finally agreed to an armistice, and this big, bloody red ball marked the date.

Now that we were sure our repatriation was imminent, Major McLaughlin instructed the senior officers, who passed his words onto the rest of us, that when "they announce the armistice, the Chinese will want to take photos of us cheering and looking happy. We are going to show no reaction whatsoever." And that's exactly what happened. The Chinese made their announcement, and we did not say a word. No smiling, no cheering. We just walked to our rooms. The Chinese had their movie cameras already, but they were unable to make any propaganda at our expense that day.

During the first days of September the Chinese finally loaded us on trucks to transport us to freedom. It was the monsoon season, it was pouring, and the trip became one more hurdle to overcome. Shortly after leaving Camp 2, we all had to get out and fill in the roadbed with rocks and dirt that a raging river had washed away. We then drove onto a railhead in central North Korea where we were put in boxcars. I slept near the open door because I wanted to see the countryside. I woke up in the middle of the night hearing this funny roaring sound, and I could feel the train shaking. I looked out and we were on a high railroad trestle over a dam. I could not see the train engine so I immediately thought we were being left there to be washed away. What had actually happened was the water was roaring beneath us and shaking the trestle so badly that they were afraid to take the locomotive across. So they pushed our cars out onto the trestle and then backed up another locomotive from the other side to pull us over it.

Before the Chinese turned us over to the UN forces, they took us to a small area outside of Kaesong, just north of P'anmunjom. It was surrounded by swamps, and the mosquitos were terrible. I had already been sick with malaria, and now I suffered another attack and became very ill. To make matters worse, the Chinese now threatened that I would not be allowed to go home because I was a Reactionary. Every day the Chinese called off a list of names, and I would walk back disappointed. I began to think they really might keep me, but on September 5 they called my name, along with the names of several other Reactionaries.

It is difficult to describe what I felt going into Freedom Village. After calling our names, the Chinese loaded us on a truck and took us down to the exchange point. When we arrived, there was an American officer and a Chinese officer, each with a clipboard to check off our names. On the American side stood a long row of MPs. They looked like monsters compared to our emaciated bodies. The American officer shook our hands, welcomed us back, and turned us over to another officer who took us on into Freedom Village. The American flag flying overhead was the most wonderful thing I had ever seen, and we eagerly saluted it. It was our flag, and we were going back to live under it.

I do not remember the exact sequence, but one of the first things we did in Freedom Village was getting rid of our clothes. We were then dusted with DDT, told to take a shower, and then received bathrobes and pajamas and another dusting of DDT. Sergeant John Clark[3] asked each of us to list any illnesses or injuries that had occurred during captivity for which we might later make a complaint to

---

3. On September 23, 2000, John J. Clark III sent William Shadish a letter detailing what he and the other returning POWs experienced in Freedom Village. Sfc. Clark helped compile medical dossiers on each of the more than 3,500 Americans who passed through Freedom Village. Unfortunately, these records were destroyed in a fire at the St. Louis Records Center in the 1960s.

the Veterans Administration. Most of the men were so anxious to get home that they feared any mention of such problems might delay their departure, so they said nothing. This reluctance hurt them years later when they tried to put together their disability claims for the Veterans Administration. In my case, I was so sick that I was moved by helicopter to a hospital somewhere south of Freedom Village, but not before a chaplain asked who among us wanted to take communion and to thank God for our safe return. I also remember someone asking me what I most wanted to eat, and I said butter. They brought out bread and butter, along with milk, meat, and ice cream.

The Eighth U.S. Army passed out this pamphlet in Freedom Village to its liberated prisoners. On the first page, Commanding General Maxwell D. Taylor wrote,

To Our Returned Comrades of the Eighth Army:

One behalf of the entire Eighth Army, I welcome you back to freedom. Throughout your captivity, your comrades of the Eighth Army have had your liberation as a constant goal of our efforts. We regret that you have had so long to wait, but from here on, I assure you that the Eighth Army will do everything in its power to speed you on your way back to your homes and families. All of our resources are at your disposal to make your stay with us as brief and as comfortable as possible. The Army knows what you have done for it and is deeply grateful to every returning veteran.

When I arrived at the field hospital, I remember being checked in and a colonel coming up and asking me, "Doctor, is there anything I can get you? Anything at all?" I told him, "I'd like to have a big drink of Scotch." I drank my Scotch and went to bed.

The doctors in the field hospital must have considered me too sick for them to treat so the next day they flew those of us in need of further care to the Tokyo Army Hospital, where I spent the next ten days. Colonel Radke, who was one of the world's foremost experts in such diseases, diagnosed me as having amoebic hepatitis (jaundice) and plasmodium vivax malaria. There is also falciparum malaria, which one finds in Africa and is deadly. The patient can tolerate plasmodium vivax malaria if he is well, although he becomes very sick with aches and pains, his eyes hurt, he runs a fever that lasts about three weeks, and the malaria tends to recur.

Colonel Radke successfully treated my amoebic hepatitis, and I thought he had taken care of my malaria as well, but it recurred in 1954 when I was doing my medical residency. I was again treated, but within a month it came back again. Finally, a lab technician came running up and said, "Look what I found." He had discovered something called fragmented plasmodia, which look like tiny red and blue targets in the blood and are found in a particular kind of malaria. Because these plasmodia were so fragmented, they had earlier been overlooked, but after their discovery I received more aggressive treatment, and I have had no attacks since then.

I was privileged to meet Major General William F. Dean while both of us were being treated in Tokyo. He had been the highest ranking POW held by the Communists. He was a great leader who always gave credit to his men, all of whom had the utmost respect for him. After the North Koreans captured him in August of 1950, he spent three years in solitary confinement, without ever seeing another American. Some of my buddies had evidently said something about me, so he invited me to his hospital room for a talk. I got to know him much better when nine of us flew home with him on a four-engine prop plane. The military had sent a special plane to fly him back to the U.S., but he rejected it saying, "I'm flying home with my men." That's the way he was.

He was very humble about his prison experiences. He told of getting to know the five men who guarded him during his captivity and even playing chess with one of them. After he was back home and living in retirement in Berkeley, he learned that this guard had defected and gone to Japan. He sent him a round-trip ticket to San Francisco, where he showed him the sights and took him to all kinds of lovely stores and restaurants. On the last night of the visit, he invited his former guard home for dinner. After they had eaten, General Dean asked him what was his most unforgettable impression of his trip. He thought he would say something about the fancy places they had visited, but what he said was, "You have no guards on the street corners." It was clearly our freedom that had most impressed him.

General William F. Dean and Captain William Shadish in New York.

I again met General Dean in New York, while I was recuperating at St. Albans Naval Hospital. It was October 26, 1953, and he was receiving New York City's Medal of Honor. After a ticker-tape parade through the streets of New York, he spoke to 1,500 cheering citizens at the City Hall Plaza. He singled out two of us in the crowd and called us to the rostrum. Then he told the crowd, "I know that in honoring me, you have in mind the men who made it possible for me to be here, those men and others who did not come back.... I heard a lot about Capt. Shadish from my fellow prisoners. A lot of our prisoners wouldn't be alive today if it hadn't been for Captain Shadish. This made me feel proud we had such medical officers in our Army. He represents the men who should be honored—not me."[4]

I was just so damn happy to be home that when we landed at Travis Air Force Base in Fairfield, California, September 20, 1953, I wasn't thinking of anything else. I had some concerns about my health, but I had confidence in the physicians who had been treating me. I had been able to talk to my wife on the phone, and was, of course, very anxious to see my two children, Will and Liz. All of them, and my mother-in-law, flew out to California to meet me. My daughter Liz was only three months old when I left so she never really knew me. When I got off the plane at Travis Air Force Base, just northwest of San Francisco, Grandma was holding her and she said, "Liz, this is your daddy." And Liz said, "I really do have a daddy!"

After a day or two at Travis Air Force Base, the military flew me to New York, where I was admitted to St. Albans Naval Hospital on Long Island. The hospital authorities had been told that a Captain Shadish was arriving, but they did not know I was a captain in the army, and not the navy. I have never experienced such a reception in my life. They even sent a special car for me. When I arrived, the Commander and everybody else were there to welcome me. I was wearing civilian clothes, but when the naval orderly put my clothes in my room, he noticed that I was only a captain in the army. "I won't tell anybody," he assured me. I lived the life of Riley in that hospital.

After I finished my initial treatment at St. Albans, I received a 90-day leave of absence. I briefly visited the Shadish family in Pennsylvania and then spent the rest of my time with my wife and children in our home in Kew Gardens on Long Island.

During those long, bitter, and deadly years while we were prisoners of war, we all dreamed of home and family and how perfect everything would be when we returned. Unfortunately, reality could ever match those dreams. Without question, our families tried to treat us with kindness and love, and we were all so very grateful to be free and back home with them, but we also soon discovered that our loved ones could never really understand what we had experienced and its aftereffects. Then, too, there was uncertainty surrounding our professional careers and the recriminations we faced.

---

4. These quotes appeared in the *Long Island Daily Press*, the *New York Times*, and the *Pittsburgh Press* on October 27, 1953.

9

RECRIMINATIONS

o o o o o o o o o o o o o o o o o o o o o o o o o o o o o o o o o o o

We have produced normally conditioned Americans trained to kill and then having no memory of having killed. (This prisoner) has been relieved of those normal American reactions of guilt and fear so he cannot give himself away.... His brain has not only been washed, it has been dry cleaned.

—Dr. Yen Lo, a fictional character in the 1962 film The Manchurian Candidate, *who programmed an American POW to be a political assassin.*

All returning prisoners were interrogated about their behavior and that of their fellow prisoners. Although this started for me just days after I was liberated while I was recuperating in the Tokyo Army Hospital, it began for most of the men on board the ships going home, and it made them very angry. There was nothing wrong with being interviewed, but these men should have been told, "We are not going to delay you from going home, regardless of what goes on here, but tell us about your experiences because after you are home, perhaps we can do something to help you." Instead, they were urged to report any examples of collaboration, often with the implication that they themselves might have collaborated or even been brainwashed. After suffering so long to remain loyal to their country, such accusations were vicious blows to their self-esteem.

Granted, there were some who collaborated with the enemy, as there have been in every war, but these were few in number. Most who did any kind of collaborating did so under severe pressure of beatings, exposure to extreme cold, starvation, humiliation, death threats, and the fear of never being allowed to go home. They were often young, untrained conscripts who had been thrown into combat without proper training. To make matter worse, they had been assigned to their combat units so recently that they did not trust their fellow soldiers. Considering the horrific conditions under which we all suffered, the surprising truth is not that there were collaborators, but that they were so few in number.

The Korean War was the first major war the United States did not win, and this was very difficult for Americans to accept. It had to be someone's fault and who better to blame than the poor enlisted men in the prison camps. For men like army psychiatrist William Mayer, who interrogated returning prisoners about things that did not exist, they made perfect scapegoats. Interestingly, neither the Marines nor the Air Force conducted comprehensive interrogations of their returning prisoners, nor did the British; only the U.S. Army did so, and I am sure that was primarily because of the damning accusations of Major William Mayer.

I've already explained that Mayer first interviewed returning prisoners in late April of 1953 during Operation Little Switch. Some of these men had been "Progressives," and in order to protect themselves they insisted that everyone had collaborated. Mayer took this information and applied it to the rest of us when we returned home four months later during Operation Big Switch. He then publicized his views in a lengthy article in *U.S. News and World Report*, during extensive lecture tours, and through tape recordings, some of which are still available. Among other things, Mayer insisted, "The behavior of too many of our soldiers in prison fell far short of the historical American standards of honor, character, loyalty, courage and personal integrity." He argued that approximately one-third of all American POWs yielded to brainwashing, which "created a substantial loss of confidence, among prisoners, in the American system, raising doubts and confusion in the prisoners' minds about themselves and their country." He also denied that harsh treatment could in any way explain negative prisoner behavior.[1] Of course, William Mayer had never been a prisoner of war.

Journalist Eugene Kinkaid also publicized alleged POW transgressions. He denigrated an entire generation when he wrote, "In every war but one that the United States has fought, the conduct of those of its service men who were held in enemy prison camps presented no unforeseen problems to the armed forces and gave rise to no particular concern in the country as a whole.... The exception was the Korean War." He agreed with Mayer that "one out of every three American prisoners in Korea was guilty of some sort of collaboration with the enemy," and that they "appeared to lose all sense of allegiance not only to their country

---

1.   William E. Mayer, "Why Did Many GI Captives Cave in?" *U. S. News and World Report*, Feb. 24, 1956.

but to their fellow prisoners." Kinkaid also argued that "the high death rate was due primarily not to Communist maltreatment but to the ignorance or the callousness of the prisoners themselves."[2] I just wish Mayer and Kinkaid could have been with us in Death Valley and Camp 5 that first winter.

The outrageous accusations of critics such as Mayer and Kinkaid predictably received tremendous media coverage, and they were reenforced in the 1962 movie, *The Manchurian Candidate*, in which all the prisoners appeared brainwashed, and by syndicated columnists such as Colonel David Hackworth, who as late as 1995 described us as a bunch of cowards who "ratted on and stole the food of their fellow inmates or allowed themselves to be used for propaganda purposes." Hackworth insisted that the men he commanded in the early 1960s "would have spit in the face of the Russkies if captured," and he promised that if we did not reaffirm the military Code of Conduct, "we can expect a rerun of the Korean War disgrace somewhere down the bloody track."[3]

For Korean War POWs, David Hackworth is a real son-of-a-bitch. He attempted to advance himself through the media at the expense of his fellow soldiers. He's precisely the kind of individual who shoots his mouth off when he's on the outside, but in a prison camp would turn out to be crap and even jeopardize the health and welfare of his fellow prisoners. I would love to have had him as my prisoner for about nine months in a place where he could not communicate with anyone, and I was not responsible for his survival. I would have had him doing anything I ordered him to do. Unfortunately, this will never happen, but I can still say, "Shame on you, David Hackworth."[4]

Sgt. Harley Coon, who was incarcerated with us in Camp 5 and who later served as President of the Korean Ex-Prisoner of War Association, wrote a scathing letter to Hackworth, which, of course, never received the kind of publicity that Hackworth's accusations did. Nevertheless, Harley Coon certainly set the record straight:

---

2.   Eugene Kinkaid, "The Study of Something New in History," *New Yorker*, 26 October 1957. This article was later expanded into a book titled *In Every War But One* (New York: W. W. Norton, 1959).

3.   *King Features Syndicate, Inc.*, January 20, 1995.

4.   David Hackworth died on May 11, 2005.

Dear Mr. Hackworth:

As a Past President of the Korean Ex-Prisoner of War Association, I take strong issue with your assessments of the Americans held as Prisoners of War in Korea.

Having spent 33 months as a Prisoner of War of the Chinese in Korea, I feel I have full authority to speak on this subject. I have never seen anyone so far off base as to what actually happened in the Prison Camps as you are....

I want to tell you of the heroics of the Prisoners in Camp 5 during a given week in April and May of 1952. There happened to be a pilot who was shot down and he was being tortured at the Chinese Headquarters. In order to free this pilot, the NCOs went on strike for a period of four days. We would not eat. We would not work and we would not move under threats of being shot and intimidated by the guards until this pilot was released and sent to Camp 2 (Officers camp)

When you say, "During the Korean War, many American POWs ratted on and stole the food of their fellow inmates, or allowed their fellow inmates to be used for propaganda purposes," you are totally out of context when you indicate all. You do not mention the time when some of us were tortured and beaten beyond human comprehension because we helped one another. Maybe you should try standing on a frozen river, holding a shingle over your head for six to eight hours because you stole this shingle to build a fire to keep our sick and wounded warm....

Well, Mr. Hackworth, when you have walked in our shoes and have endured the hardships that the Americans held in the Korean Prisoner of War Camps did, then, and only then, would you have a right to access what really happened....

An apology is due to all Prisoners of War who have sacrificed their freedom.[5]

Another recent writer who resurrected old myths was Raymond Lech, whose 2000 *Broken Soldiers* argued, "The majority of the captive Americans did practically everything their North Korean and Chinese captors told them to do." Lech went on to blame a fear of death and slow starvation for prisoner complicity: "After they had cleared the body of its meat, after they had living skeletons in their cages, they began to 'cleanse' the mind.... It was at this point, in April 1951, that great numbers of officers and enlisted, young and old, white and black, turned their backs on the West and began to embrace the enemy. There were exceptions, but they were the minority."[6] This too was another gross distor-

---

5.   Harley Coon letter sent to David Hackworth, King Features Syndicate, Inc., February 8, 1995.

6.   Lech, *Broken Soldiers*, 3.

tion of the truth. I can assure Raymond Lech, who refused to interview former prisoners because he believed their memories to be untrustworthy after the passage of too much time, that regardless of our ages, we who were prisoners, and only we, are fully capable of bearing witness to what actually happened in those dreadful camps.

A few writers did defend the returning prisoners; unfortunately, their books and articles never received the kind of media attention that those of our critics did. William Lindsay White's *The Captives of Korea* rejected the idea that "an alarming number of our POWs disgraced themselves," while insisting that "our prisoners were treated with a savagery unequaled in modern times.[7] U.S. Air Force Intelligence psychologist Al Biderman, whose *March to Calumny* also attacked the idea that the POWs had disgraced themselves, argued, "The prisoners became the subject of another type of propaganda—propaganda by Americans, about Americans, directed to Americans." Biderman emphasized that by blaming the victims, our critics absolved the Koreans and Chinese Communists of any responsibility for the more than 3,000 American prisoners who died because of their mistreatment.[8]

There was also a group of twenty-one prominent scholars who signed a statement titled "To Set Straight the Korean POW Episode," which concluded, "Instances of moral weakness, collaboration with the enemy, and failure to take care of fellow soldiers in Korea did not occur more frequently than in other wars where comparable conditions of physical and psychological hardship were present. Indeed, such instances appear to have been less prevalent than historical experience would lead us to expect."[9]

7.   William L. White, *The Captives of Korea: An Unofficial White Paper on the Treatment of War Prisoners; Our Treatment of Theirs; Their Treatment of Ours* (New York: Scribner's, 1957), 265.

8.   Albert Biderman, *March to Calumny: The Story of the American POWs in the Korean War* (New York: Macmillan, 1963), 1, 5-6, 101, 188. A year earlier, Biderman published "Dangers of Negative Patriotism" in the *Harvard Business Review* (November-December, 1962) to alert the Business Community to the many distortions of the POW experience. Interestingly, Biderman contended that most academics did not want to produce scholarly rebuttals to the charges of prisoner malfeasance because they considered the attacks themselves to be unscholarly.

9.   Edgar H. Schein drew up the statement "To Set Straight the Korean POW Episode," which was reprinted in the aforementioned "Dangers of Negative Patriotism." Among the signers were Gordon W. Allport, Harvard University; Colonel William H. Anderson, Office of the Surgeon General; David Riesman, Harvard University; and esteemed military historian, S. L. A. Marshall.

In a June 24, 1954 presentation to the American Medical Association titled "Medical Experiences in Communist POW Camps in Korea," the five of us doctors who survived captivity responded to the charges that American prisoners were guilty of mass misbehavior or that they somehow were to blame for their own deaths:

> Virtually all of the deaths in the Communist prisoner of war camps were caused directly or indirectly by starvation, exposure, and the harassment by the enemy.... During the first month or two of captivity most of the deaths occurred among the wounded. During the succeeding three to five months most the men died either from pneumonia or dysentery, or from a combination of these two. After the first five or six months of captivity the majority of deaths occurred among persons suffering from pellagra or beriberi. During one five-month period there were between 5 and 28 deaths per day in one camp in North Korea. None of these men had illnesses that would have caused death had they been under normal conditions.[10]

---

10. This presentation to the American Medical Association was later reprinted in the *Journal of the American Medical Association*, Sept. 11, 1954, 121. The complete text of this presentation can be found on page 124 in the Appendix.

Early in 1954, Surgeon General George E. Armstrong honored the five
American U.S. Army physicians who survived their Korean War captivity
for the care and encouragement they gave to their fellow prisoners.
From left to right: Major Clarence L. Anderson, Capt. Gene N. Lam,
Major General Armstrong, Capt. William R. Shadish, Capt. Sidney Esen-
sten, and Major Alexander M. Boysen.

In the final analysis, the Army's case against collaborators fell of its own
weight. Out of its initial 900 targeted cases, the Army considered only 425 for
court-martial, a figure it later reduced to 82, before a review body dropped it to
47.

Of these 47 men, 14 came to trial and only 11 were convicted. One served ten
years for striking an officer and mistreating other prisoners, and another had his
murder charge overturned. The remaining nine were convicted of some form of
collaboration, but these charges were considered so ambiguous or controversial
that no one was incarcerated for more than five years.[11]

---

11.   See John Wiant, *et al.*, "POW Collaboration Charges Exploded," *Register & Defense
Times* (April 16, 1960), 9, and Lech, *Broken Soldiers*, 264-276.

◆   ◆   ◆

I personally was interrogated several times, before I received my final clearance. Those of us who were career soldiers could not even be promoted until we removed this cloud of suspicion hanging over our heads, and this often took months. In my case, it was more than a year before I was fully exonerated, including the lifting of "administrative restrictions," and was promoted to major. Many of the details of this long and stressful process remained unknown to me until I was able to procure my military file in 1992 under the Freedom of Information Act.

The investigative process actually began on September 5, 1953, which was three days before I was officially liberated, when the Department of the Army's G-2 conducted a "Criminal Check" on me with the FBI, the result of which was "No criminal record."

My initial interrogations began on September 16, 1953 at the Tokyo Army Hospital, where I was convalescing under the care of Dr. Radke. This was only eleven days after liberation, and I recall very little about these days because I was still suffering the effects of hepatitis and malaria. The summarizing "Agent Report,"signed by Philip C. Armknecht of the 116th CIC Detachment, made it clear that the interrogators also included a Captain Harold S. Hess and a Stephen C. Balough, both from the 441st CIC Detachment, and medical intelligence officers from Armed Forces Far East Command and the Eighth Army, all of whom served under something called the Japan Joint Intelligence Processing Board (JIPB). However, the two men who made the most damning comments were identified only by their initials. The resultant report, which included both true and untrue information, concluded that I was "a tentative security risk."[12]

I was asked about having treated the Chinese officer Kuo Tsien-tsu in Death Valley, which I had indeed done. I told the JIPB representatives that I considered my treatment of Tsien-tsu to be in accordance with my Hippocratic Oath as a physician, and that I hoped to trade my services for medicine for our extremely sick prisoners. In addition, Major Burt Coers, who was my immediate superior in Death Valley, had given his approval. The interrogators also suggested that Gene

---

12.   "Agent Report," Shadish Official Report, File No: MN-LP (18 January 1956) was a summary of the JIPB's Tokyo interrogations of September 16-18, 1953. William Shadish received this file under the Freedom of Information Act. See also G2-SPD Memo, dated 13 April 1954, which was also part of the official Shadish file.

Lam and I had volunteered to move into a room near Kuo Tsien-tsu, but the truth was Kuo Tsien-tsu had ordered us to do so.

The JIPB Report also stated that I, along with 400 other prisoners, had signed an anti-American statement entitled "May We Be Heard?" Although I had signed no such document, my name, along with the others, had been read on a March 30, 1951 Radio Peiping's English-language propaganda broadcast that quoted me as saying in a letter home, "The attitude of our captors has been most amicable. Dearest ..., advise everyone through the press and public officials to urge a peaceful settlement of this Korean conflict. All foreign troops should be withdrawn from Korea immediately." The JIPB report did admit, however, that there was no record of any such letter being sent to my wife and that the letters she was asked to submit to the investigators who had gone to our home to question her were "devoid of propaganda matter."

In addition, the JIPB wanted to know why in late 1951 approximately forty of us in Camp 2 had sent messages home via a recording machine. After the Chinese assured us there were no strings attached, we had agreed to do so because we welcomed the opportunity to reassure our loved ones that we were all right. However, the Chinese did not inform us that what we recorded would go out to the world in the December 16, 1951 edition of the English-language *Shanghai News*. In my case, this is what appeared in the *Shanghai News*:

> Capt. William (Bill) R. Shadish, 0-976688, to his wife, Mrs. W. R. Shadish, 135-16 Horace Harding Blvd, Flushing, New York: Since I have received no mail from you to date, the Chinese Volunteers, who had captured me in Dec. 1950, have given me the opportunity to make this broadcast message. I am in good health and am being treated well. I want to wish you and the children, Bill and Mary Elizabeth, a very Merry Christmas and Happy New Year. I love you very much.[13]

The JIPB Report also quoted a fellow prisoner accusing me of signing a petition in hopes of getting personal medical aid, which I certainly had never done. Then, in one of its positive statements, the Report quoted my thoughts on Communism: "The Communists are a bunch of thieves, robbers and murderers. Communism breaks every one of the Ten Commandments. It could never work in the U. S. by choice of the people because it is against all of our principles."[14]

---

13. *Ibid.*
14. *Ibid.*

The CIC's Stephen C. Balough was very supportive in his concluding comments: "Shadish was completely cooperative and did not appear to be withholding any information. He indicated that he would like to be interviewed by PSYWAR and give his opinions on mental reactions and his opinions for the actions of some of the PW'S. Recommend no further counter-intelligence interrogation."[15]

Another interrogator, however, who was identified in the report only by the initials GRH, wrote, "If this man had been as faithful to his oath of allegiance as an Army Officer as he claims he was to the Hippocratic Oath, he probably would not have received favors from the Chinese, and would probably be able to furnish more and better counter intelligence information to his government. Recommend no clearance. Cat: C and D."[16]

The comments of the chairman of the JIPB, who also was identified only by his initials HMF, were equally negative: "Having lived so close to the Flagpole and responsible for sick call for our PW's, Subject has surprisingly little to offer from a counter intelligence standpoint. He accepted favors, but said he was ordered to do so. His oath may cover some of the activities, but it has exposed him as a collaborator. Recommend further exploitation [sic] upon return to Conus. Cleared for departure. Cat: C and D."

Receiving a C rating meant I "was thought to have collaborated with the enemy in a treasonable manner" and that further investigation was needed. Category D included individuals who were thought to have personal knowledge of war crimes and/or atrocities.[17]

My next contact with military intelligence occurred January 14–15, 1954, while I was convalescing at Walter Reed Army Medical Center. Both medical and military personnel interviewed me in a large room at the Pentagon. The doctors and dentists pretty much restricted their questions to medical problems. Then came the intelligence services. Some of their questions were germane, but others seemed to accept the myth of massive collaboration and in many instances were hostile. I tried to answer as comprehensively as I could, but some of them did not seem satisfied with my answers. For instance, when I was asked about the structure of Chinese military units, I told them I didn't know a damn thing about this. One of the intelligence officers said, "It's pretty obvious you are not telling

---

15. *Ibid.*
16. *Ibid.*
17. *Ibid.*

us everything you know." That was very inappropriate because I knew little about military matters.

They also asked me about a June 1951 petition I had signed. I explained that the Chinese had called on all the officers of Camp 5 to sign the so-called Stockholm Peace Appeal, which eventually was sent to the United Nations and a Stockholm-based Peace Conference. The Chinese insisted the petition be debated among the captured officers, and, after some three days, all but eight had signed. Then Major John MacLaughlin and six of the others agreed to sign, which left only me. A Chinese political cadre eventually came up to me and said, "You are the only one who hasn't signed, and you will sign it." I have already noted how much I admired Major MacLaughlin, who later became a two-star general in the Marine Corps. I figured if he signed it, I would as well. McLaughlin's behavior was always proper, but he realized that if we did not "cooperate" and sign, our troops would not receive any proper food or care. I realized he was right so I became the last to sign it. MacLaughlin reassured us the people back home would understand, and the Marines, except for the Colonel Frank Schwable case,[18] did not hassle their troops after they returned to the States, and neither did the Air Force. It was only the Army. As a matter of fact, the prisoners who arrived in Camp 2 toward the end of our captivity told us they could say anything if it would help them stay alive and it would not be held against them.

After answering all their questions, I was given the opportunity to write a long description of my military and POW experiences, much of which I have incorporated in the combat and POW chapters of this memoir.[19] I also turned over the list of names I had smuggled out of the prison camps of the more than 300 prisoners whose deaths I could verify.

---

18. Col. Frank Schwable was a Naval Academy graduate and a highly decorated World War II Marine fighter pilot. After being shot down on July 2, 1952, he spent months in solitary confinement, suffering severe physical and mental deprivation. Four months later, a broken man "confessed" to participating in "germ warfare" and other crimes. His "confession" was written and rewritten and then edited by the Chinese and released to the world in January 1953. After Col. Schwable returned home, a Naval and Marine panel of four high-ranking officers cleared him of all charges, stating he had "resisted this torture to the limit of his ability to resist." See, Raymond Lech, *Broken Soldiers*, 165-166, 221, 240-241.

19. A copy of this report, titled *Report Prepared by SHADISH, William R., Captain, Medical Corps, U.S. Army, O-976688, for the Surgeon General, U.S. Army*, was obtained under the Freedom of Information Act.

In addition to this lengthy biographical description, I wrote a two-page state-ment titled "Witnessed Statement," which began, "I, Captain William R. Shad-ish, … having been duly advised that I need not make this statement and that it may be used against me in any proceeding, civil or criminal, declare that the fol-lowing statement is given freely and voluntarily, without promise or benefit, or threat or use of force or duress, do proceed to state as follows."[20] I went on to recount what I remembered about a man accused of murdering another prisoner and the major who had told us in Camp 2 that his superiors had ordered us to cooperate with the Chinese. I described hearing shots after prisoners dropped out on the march to Death Valley and how a man named Pritchett had been mur-dered by the Chinese for escaping and being critical of the Communists. I also wrote about being required to sign death certificates in Camp 5 for those prison-ers who died in captivity, but refusing to sign any statement that these prisoners had died of syphilis, as the Chinese ordered me to do. I also mentioned a Major McGhee being sentenced to six months in solitary confinement for reading a confession in which he stated that Communism was false and that he didn't believe in it. Finally, I described a questionnaire that asked prisoners to write down the names, addresses, financial status, income, and political leanings of our families and close friends.

I was contacted again by G-2 on April 27, 1954, out of which emerged a vari-ety of increasingly positive reports. In a Memo dated May 28, 1954, Lt Colonel Charles M. Trammell, Jr. wrote, "Review of the evidence now available indicates that this case is not appropriate for presentation to the Department of the Army Prisoner of War Collaboration Board for consideration of court-martial action…. The subject conducted himself creditably with no showing of collaboration."[21]

Attached to this memo were three items: Biographical Sketch, Summary of Evidence, and my RECAP-K file. The Summary of Evidence repeated the claim of the initial Joint Intelligence Processing Board in Japan that I should have had more counterintelligence information to give them and more knowledge of vari-ous atrocities. My response was that I could not report on things I had not wit-nessed, and that I was more than willing to provide detailed descriptions of how horribly our Communist captors had treated us on the march to Death Valley and in the camps themselves. Then, strangely enough, this same interim report

---

20. "Witnessed Statement," January 15, 1954. Obtained under the Freedom of Infor-mation Act.

21. "Office Memorandum, United States Government to Capt Chalupsky, Special Counsel, RECAP-K to Chief, Disposition Section," May 28, 1954. Obtained under the Freedom of Information Act.

stated, "His fellow prisoners do not accuse him of collaboration, only name him as being the officer in charge of camp sanitation."

The most important information in the Summary of Evidence report were the comments of returning prisoners who had mentioned my name during their own interrogations. Of the ninety statements only four could be considered derogatory, one of which stated I had signed a petition and another that I had circulated a petition. One of these men was bitter because he had not been among those to whom I had given medicine in Death Valley. One of the others said I had lived outside the POW compound in Death Valley while treating Kuo Tsien-tsu, and the fourth one stated I had lived at the hospital to facilitate my duties. One of them also said I had frequently reported to camp officials, which probably referred to the several times I pleaded with the Chinese for medicine and better living conditions for my patients.

Suspicion and the search for incriminating evidence characterized the interrogations of all returning POWs. The details may have differed but the overall intention was to vilify each and every one of us. This was reprehensible, and especially when those being interrogated were encouraged to repeat any negative stories or rumors they might have heard about their fellow prisoners.[22]

We were all judged guilty until proven innocent, so it obviously angered me to hear disparaging remarks about my character, especially when they were not true. Fortunately, these negative comments were effectively countered by the testimony of the overwhelming majority of my fellow prisoners. I realize it sounds self-serving to include such comments, but I do so to illustrate the kind of defense each of us had to make. I also want to express by appreciation to these men who, in spite of the political climate of the times, did not hesitate to speak out.

Captain Carroll Wright testified that I had tried to work with the Chinese in hope of obtaining more medical supplies, but only after receiving the permission of superior officers to do so, and that I had stopped because the Chinese never fulfilled their promises. He also testified that I had been thrown into the hole for saying that "copulation must be the number one sport in China" during a discus-

---

22. The army's interrogations of the returning prisoners often extended to subjects far beyond collaboration. In one such example, Richard Bassett was questioned about Howard Adams, one of the twenty-one so-called "Turncoats," who after liberation chose China rather than return to the United States. Bassett was asked if Adams was a homosexual, mentally subnormal, depraved, or smoked marijuana. Richard Bassett, with Lewis H. Carlson, *And the Wind Blew Cold; The Story of an American POW in North Korea* (Kent, Ohio: The Kent State University Press, 2002), 109.

sion involving the large population of China. Finally, and most important, he said that some of the sick prisoners who had not received medicine from me in Death Valley, when I had to make a determination on who needed it the most, had become angry and spread lies that I had sold medicine to the enlisted men.

Several men testified that I had been punished because of my anti-Communist views. Air Force First Lt William G. Boswell said I was "punished because of organized resistance to disrupt the Chinese indoctrination program." First Lt Paul O'Dowd put it more bluntly: "Shadish went to jail for his outspoken hatred of communism." Lt. Col. Roy Gramling Jr. said I had "helped unify the men" in Death Valley and that I "was definitely anti-Communist." Major Andrew Fedenets testified that I had received a thirty-day confinement sentence "for general harassment and non-cooperating with the Chinese." Air Force Captain Frederick P. Pelser described how my refusal to salute after being appointed squad leader in Camp 2 had resulted in my being placed in solitary confinement. Captain Lawrence V. Bach stated, "Shadish opposed the communists in their efforts to influence the prisoners (and) was considered to be the leader of the opposition to communism and ... our captors." Air Force Major David F. MacGhee remembered I had been "relieved of all sick call duties at Camp 5 for insisting on medical supplies."

Sfc. Vernet L. Fetter testified, "Shadish was a medical officer who helped save many lives at Camp 5." M/Sgt Edgar J. McIntyre stated, "Shadish did much to help the prisoners (and) a petition was circulated to have an award given to him." Sgt. Oscar Best also recommended me for an award for "helping the sick prisoners at Camp 5." Air Force S./Sgt Richard Jones reported, "The amount of good he has done is immeasurable.... He always did his utmost to restore the men's confidence in themselves.... He constantly struggled every hour to help the sick and wounded and is responsible for many men being alive today. He was respected and admired by all men in camp.... He is the outstanding man I met in prison camp."

In a lengthy letter to the Adjutant General, M/Sgt Cecil J. Thompson wrote, "Disregarding their threats and punishment, Dr. Shadish would visit the sick men each day. He did not have any medicine to give to them except the love of one soldier to another and his superb devotion to a fellow soldier. The men were so sick and weak that they wanted to die and were only lying there until death would take them out of their agony. At this point of suffering Dr. Shadish would visit these men and explain to them why they should want to live and what they had to live for."[23]

On April 13, 1954, in response to an official letter I wrote on March 22, requesting renewal of my active duty category, the Assistant Chief of Staff, G-2, Department of the Army, stated "no objection from a security standpoint." A Memo attached to his declaration stated,

> Captain Shadish was a leader of the opposition to the Communists and their indoctrination program, who had been placed in the hole because of his refusal to obey an order to salute the Chinese. On another occasion he was given a jail sentence for his non-cooperative attitude toward the Communists. Shadish, a doctor, saved many lives and was commended by his fellow prisoners for his unselfish devotion to the sick POWs.... . During the darkest days at the PW camp he raised the morale and the spirit of the men, gave news and information to the PsW [sic], sat up through the night with sick PsW, and offered his rations to those who needed it.... Action has been initiated to lift the administrative restriction placed on Shadish.[24]

A November 4, 1954 memo, designated only as "Phase I and II Interrogations,"reported that "a check of the files of the security division revealed one derogatory excerpt and others of a possible derogatory nature," but that further study "showed it to be in error. The other excerpts appear to be innocuous in the light of testimony from other officers. Shadish has been given a security clearance by the Security Division and has had his category extended and promotion approved."[25]

This process of clearing my name lasted fourteen long months before I knew that no one was looking over my shoulder or questioning my patriotism. In the meantime, I was doing everything I could to resume my career as a physician in the U.S. Army.

---

23. All these comments appeared in the aforementioned "Summary of Evidence," Office Memorandum, May 28, 1954.

24. Shadish official file, G2-SPD, April 13, 1954, Obtained under the Freedom of Information Act..

25. Untitled Memo, June 23, 1954. Included in the Shadish File obtained under the Freedom of Information Act.

10

PHYSICAL AND PSYCHOLOGICAL REPERCUSSIONS

o o o o o o o o o o o o o o o o o o o o o o o o o o o o o o o o o o

Every former Korean War POW returned home with a weakened heart, weakened bones, demolished teeth, and a generalized weakened nervous system, along with a smashed psychological ego.

—William Shadish, letter to the VA's Office of Planning and Program Evaluation, June 4, 1979

You could be the most psychologically put together person that ever walked the face of the earth, but it is my belief that you could develop PTSD given enough stress.

—Dr. Glenn P. Smith, clinical psychologist at the James A. Haley Veterans Hospital in Tampa, Florida

Shortly after my final security clearance in November of 1954, I was contacted by Louis Columbo, an aid to Senator William E. Jenner's Internal Security Subcommittee. Columbo asked for recommendations on how to handle possible future Communist indoctrination sessions of captured American personnel. Among other things, I urged that at a young age all Americans become more aware of the workings of democracy and the evils of communism. I also recommended a specific Code of Conduct that "clearly explained to each and every individual ... that regardless of status as a prisoner, the soldier is bound by oath to remain a soldier and no statement or action to the contrary by the enemy can in any way change this."[1]

Technically, all a prisoner of war should offer is his name, rank, and serial number, but this is not realistic. We should teach those captured to hold out as long as they can and make every effort not to sign anything. The goal is to tell one's captors nothing, and never to jeopardize the welfare of a fellow prisoner, but there also are times when you have to use common sense. The Chinese were not after military information, except perhaps when a man was first captured, and even then you could circumvent their questions by bluffing and lying. The Chinese were using their interrogations to try and make us question our government and the American way of life.

In 1955, President Dwight Eisenhower approved a new Code of Conduct that reflected some of the suggestions I had sent Senator Jenner's subcommittee. The Eisenhower Code began, "I am an American fighting man, responsible for my actions, and dedicated to the principles which made my country free. I will trust in my God and in the United States of America." The Code then instructed,

> Each member of the armed forces liable to capture shall be provided with specific training and instruction designed to better equip him to counter and withstand all enemy efforts against him, and shall be fully instructed as to the behavior and obligations expected of him during combat or captivity.... When questioned, should I become a prisoner of war, I am bound to give only name, rank, service number, and date of birth. I will evade answering further questions to the utmost of my ability. I will make no oral or written statements disloyal to my country and its allies or harmful to their cause.[2]

Of course, to make this Code work, we must fully educate our soldiers before they go into combat in terms of what it means to be an American and what their status will be as a POW. As I explained in my letter to the Senate Internal Security Subcommittee, "In many instances, the men in prison with me were almost totally deficient of a working knowledge of their own government, much less that of the enemy." I also emphasized that a POW must understand that he remains a member of the U.S. Army, although the Communists tried to convince us that such was not the case. Finally, I stressed that organizational integrity, from the top down, was all important to avoid a physical and mental breakdown among the men. The rigid command structure of the Turkish POWs, from the highest officer to the lowest soldier, was a good example.[3]

---

1.   Letter to Mr. Louis Columbo, Senate Internal Security Subcommittee, November 9, 1954. The full text of this letter can be found on page 156 in the Appendix.
2.   The Code of Conduct originated in Eisenhower's Executive Order 10631, which was released on August 17, 1955.

◆   ◆   ◆

I am not sure what could have been done to make our transition easier. While we were in Freedom Village, we were asked, "Do you have any problems you want to talk about?" Naturally, after all we had gone through, the only thing we wanted to do was go home, so of course we did not admit to any personal problems, even though every one of us had suffered physical and emotional injuries.

The long-term effects of our physical problems would affect us the rest of our lives. My own health was typical. I have already mentioned my recurring bouts of malaria. I also had dengue fever, which the men called break-bone fever. It only lasts for about a week, but it feels like someone has broken all your bones. I had dysentery so bad in Death Valley that Gene Lam thought I was going to die. I have cardiac problems, acute arthritis, diabetes, loss of hearing, neuritis in my extremities from vitamin B deficiencies, and numbness in my extremities from having suffered frozen feet and fingers, which is exacerbated by cold weather.[4]

Bouts of hepatitis and various worm infestations were common among prisoners, and we all suffered ordinary diarrhea and scabies. The physical stress on our bodies, particularly from malnutrition, was devastating. We lacked the necessary protein for continued survival, and each of us lost approximately 50 percent of our body weight. Forced physical work with diminished body weight and muscle mass and poor bone homeostasis because of a lack of vitamins and minerals made us vulnerable to bone and joint diseases, particularly of the back. Most prisoners suffered some form of neuritis, and night blindness and hearing loss were common because of severe vitamin deficiencies. Pellagra, which is marked by skin eruptions, digestive and nervous disturbances, and eventual mental deterioration and even death, was triggered by niacin deficiency.[5]

All Korean War prisoners had some form of beriberi from which they continue to suffer neurological and heart damage. For example, arrhythmia of the heart can be a direct consequence of beriberi. Only recently has the VA agreed that former POWs suffering cardiac failure will now be covered under the beriberi heart provision. In addition, dental disease was rampant and the effects were

---

3.   Columbo letter, Nov. 9, 1954.

4.   For a comprehensive treatment of the effects of below freezing weather, see "Cold Weather Injuries," beginning on page 142 in the Appendix.

5.   For a comprehensive treatment of the consequences of vitamin deficiencies, see "Vitamin and Mineral Deficiencies and the Resultant Diseases," beginning on page 139 in the Appendix.

often permanent. Diabetes also is more common in Korean War POWs than in the general public.

All of us suffer some degree of traumatic arthritis. Addressing a large audience of Korean Ex-POWs in 1986, I asked for a show of hands of those who had experienced no back or joint problems. Only four men raised their hands. Many of us had been beaten and forced to carry heavy loads on skeletal bodies resulting in trauma to the joints. Arthritis can also be a manifestation of mineral deprivation. For example, the calcium deficiencies we all suffered in the camps can lead to osteoporosis of the bones and deformation of the joints. In addition, repeated microtrauma of joint surfaces of grossly malnourished individuals with poor muscular support of joints results in an abnormal motion and trauma to the joints. There is also something called amoebic arthritis, caused by amoebic dysentery. It disappears with clearance of the dysentery but, as with any joint inflamation, there may be later manifestations.

In my mind, everyone's liver has been damaged, allowing former POWs to succumb more easily to any disease affecting the liver, including alcoholism. Many of the men drink too much, but they also started out with considerable liver damage because so many had contracted Type A hepatitis. An individual can function with a loss of 70 percent of these liver cells, but when that percentage diminishes, he is living on the edge.

Many of these problems could not have been diagnosed or even anticipated when we were liberated, but they certainly manifested themselves in our later lives. Similarly, no one could have measured the decrease in our bodies' reserves at the time of liberation. Large doses of vitamins and minerals might have helped, and clearly a nutritious diet was very important for our physical recovery. Physically, the former prisoners retain the damage, and when the aging process eats away at the remainder of their reserves, the symptoms become much more obvious.

When we compare the life spans of former prisoners to ordinary civilians, the results superficially look very close. However, this is to compare the hardened, extraordinary group of men who survived captivity to a general population that never experienced similar physical or mental trauma. To make a fair comparison, one would have to find a comparable extraordinary group in the general population and then compare respective life spans, but how does one do that? This is a difficult concept to get across, but we do know that POWs have diminished life expectancies.

I maintain that any man who has been a prisoner of war for any extended period of time that includes severe emotional trauma, gross deprivation of food, extreme exposure to the elements, and life-threatening diseases without proper medication, as was experienced in the North Korean prison camps, is going to be seriously disabled later in life. This is difficult to understand when seeing former prisoners just after liberation, but examining them again after a period of time makes it clear that they are physically and psychologically different from their civilian counterparts.

◆　　　◆　　　◆

I am sure more could have been done for the mental aspects of our recovery. Before Post-Traumatic Stress Disorder (PTSD) became recognized in the early 1980s, we considered mental complaints to be just bitching. All returning prisoners are going to have some form of PTSD, and the wives are the number one verifiers of this. Their husbands say, "Hey, I'm doing fine; I don't have any problems," but the wives will tell you a different story. The men are often too proud or ashamed to tell anyone what they are going through. They insist, "Hey, there's nothing wrong with me. These other guys? Well, they're just not tough enough."[6]

It is important to understand that former prisoners have been conditioned to react in this manner. In order to survive in a POW camp where the enemy has total control, they had to protect themselves as much as possible. They could not lose their temper and physically attack their captors because to do so could lead to sudden and certain death. As a result, they learned to control their anger and rage by building a shell around themselves and crawling into it every time a stressful situation occurred, and these occurred daily. POWs thus learned to "clam up" or pull into a shell and withdraw from the world they once knew to avoid further punishment. They learned this as a matter of survival, and they learned it well and used it constantly. When they came home, they could not abandon this learned or conditioned behavior. Wives verify this when they say, "He is impossible to reach; he is emotionally numb."

There is also survivor guilt, triggered by the memory of buddies who did not make it, anger or shame at having been captured at all, and rage at one's captors and those of their own countrymen who accused them of collaboration and general misbehavior. These men are going to recall things they do not want to

---

6.　Dr. Shadish spoke out on this issue in a speech at a Conference on PTSD at the Veterans' Administration Medical Center in San Francisco in August 1991, a copy of which can be found in the Appendix, beginning on page 146.

remember, or they are going to attempt to bury negative thoughts, which will only make matters worse. None of these feelings lessen over the years. Indeed, they often intensify, creating a profound loss of power and self-esteem. If left unexpressed, they can wreak havoc by coming out in insidious ways, through spouse and child abuse, alcohol and drug addiction, severe self-neglect, and even suicide.

Years of psychic numbing have forced many former POWs to live in a world of silence, unable to tell others about their experiences. Some have never even told their wives. It is important that these men discover that this mental anguish is not happening only to them, but to other men as well. Group sessions become very important because when one man opens up, others are more willing to talk about similar problems. And when a former prisoner says he does not need help, someone, preferably a former POW, has to tell him, "The hell you don't. We all need help." They also need to understand that no matter how sympathetic health care workers are, and many of them try very hard, if they were not prisoners of war in one of the Far Eastern camps, there is no way they can ever fully understand what these men have experienced.

Those administering therapy sessions must pose questions about anger, an inability to communicate and problem-solve, depression and mood swings, destructive habits, and nightmares, followed by waking up in a sweat with pounding hearts and feelings of terror. It is important to draw out these men because most will resist or refuse to say anything voluntarily.

The wives must also be a part of this healing process. The men might first attend a few meetings among themselves, but they should then be asked to bring their wives as well. If wives know what their husbands are going through, they can be of great help.

The children also suffer when former POW fathers do not come to grips with their problems. These fathers typically insist on discipline. They remember that without their total commitment to discipline in the camps, they would not have made it. So they say to themselves, "I want my children to be just as tough as I was so they can make it through anything. They must live a disciplined, structured life in case they get into a similar situation." Not surprisingly, many children rebel against such demands, which in turn sets up a difficult environment for parent-child relationships.

The general population also needs to be educated about what combat troops, and especially POWs, have gone through. We all remember when the general public thought all returning Vietnam veterans were crazies who were likely to grab a gun and start shooting people, just as they thought all Korean War POWs were brainwashed collaborators. Many news reports and a number of Hollywood movies contributed to such distorted thinking.

For years I had heard about the 1962 film *The Manchurian Candidate*. When I finally rented it, my reaction was, my God, how did they dream that up? The movie had nothing to do with what went on inside the camps. It showed the men being turned into zombies. More than anything else after I got home, I emphasized that the Chinese did attempt to indoctrinate and even brainwash us but that they were not successful. Every day they tried to flood our minds with all kinds of propaganda and nonsense. We talked about this in camp, and I don't think anybody bought into what they were saying. A typical response was, "Awww, we have to go listen to all that bullshit again." Hollywood certainly did not care about the truth. It was much more interested in making money by exploiting the myths about us.

No one has ever made a movie about how Korean War prisoners were actually treated.[7] Instead of collaboration scenarios, a realistic film could have depicted the horrific conditions under which we were forced to survive. Such a film might have done much to change how the American people thought about us. Hollywood always tries to reduce the story to one or two individuals, but with us it was the enormity of more than 3,000 prisoners losing their lives because of the conditions under which the Chinese and North Korean Communists forced us to live.

◆   ◆   ◆

I believe I have pretty well handled my own PTSD, especially after I became more aware of what captivity had done to me. POWs had to learn to control themselves. We may have hated our captors, but we could not just fly off the handle and physically attack them. I recall during one of my stays in the hole getting into an argument with a Chinese guard and almost slugging him. Mike Lorenzo was in the next hole, and he later told me, "Doc, I was afraid you were going to hit him." We had to learn not to react physically. Instead, we had to withdraw completely into a kind of cocoon, not allowing anything to get to us. This meant

---

7.   Hollywood produced relatively few films about the Korean War POWs. In addition to *The Manchurian Candidate* (1962), other movies were *Prisoner of War (1954)*, *The Bamboo Prison* (1954), *The Rack* (1956), and *Time Limit* (1957), all of which dealt with collaboration. Interestingly, The Vietnam War, whose POWs numbered only 766 in contrast to the 7,140 Korean War prisoners, inspired more than fifty feature films, many of which included former POWs such as Rambo hellbent on revenge. In contrast, the many World War II POW films dealt almost exclusively with escape.

shutting out everything, sometimes even buddies. Unfortunately, that technique stayed with us and was very difficult to break.

After I went into private practice in Redding, California, in 1966, I always had very positive relations with my patients, but I experienced difficulties getting along with some of my medical colleagues and administrators. I was very unyielding in my opinions and found it difficult to accept contrary ideas or tolerate anything that I considered to be improper or wrong for my patients. I would talk to hospital officials in no uncertain terms, and that never went over very well. I think the medical community was sort of afraid of me, as if I were a volcano about to erupt. I would not have reacted that way before becoming a POW. As I look back on this, it was wrong not to accept people for what they were, and I should have worked harder at establishing mutual trust.

Professional therapy can help, and many men eventually responded to support groups found in Veterans Administration Medical Centers throughout the country. Nevertheless, for a long time, I did not want to go to any kind of POW meeting because doing so would have reminded me of too many Chinese and North Korean atrocities. I have already mentioned that I had trouble getting started writing this book because I did not want to relive all those painful memories. There were also times when I found it difficult to concentrate, but I think I've been fortunate not to have PTSD as severely as many of the other men. My blessing in camp was being a doctor who was able to help people. I know that made a big difference. Most of the time I could not do all that much, but at least I did not have to sit and stare at the wall.

Fortune smiled on me when I married a wonderful woman, Karen Philips, in 1972. Karen taught me how to come out of my shell. At first, when a stressful situation occurred, I withdrew. I would not speak to Karen or anyone else, which is not healthy behavior. Fortunately, Karen had the patience and commitment to draw me out of my self-imposed silence. Other men have not been so fortunate and remain resistant to ridding themselves of their shell. They do not acknowledge that they actually behave this way or fully understand that such behavior is abnormal. It took me, a physician, twenty years to recognize this problem in myself.

For some of the men, their PTSD became worse after they retired. Many of them had managed to lose themselves in their careers, using their work in the same way alcoholics use drink to blot out everything else in their lives. Some were also actual alcoholics, but during their working years they drank only in the evening. After they retired, they had too much time on their hands, and many of the old demons returned to torment them. One need only ask a recently retired former POW if he has begun suffering more nightmares.

Fortunately, that did not occur with me. Building and caring for a very large rose garden and becoming immersed in fossil hunting have kept me busy. In fact, now, at age 83, I often lie awake nights thinking, I've got so much to do, and I'm not going to get it all done before I die.

POSTSCRIPT

After my convalescence at St. Alban's Naval Hospital and a ninety-day leave of absence, I had to figure out what I was going to do with the rest of my life. At first I considered getting out of the service, but when I thought about how far I had fallen behind in my profession during my more than three years in Korea, I decided that the best thing I could do was to stay in the army and update my training.

When I went to Korea, I wanted to be a general practitioner, but after what I had seen in combat and in the prison camps, I thought I might want to become a trauma surgeon. I said as much to Surgeon General Leonard Heaton, and in January 1954 he assigned me to Walter Reed Army Hospital. Colonel Thalman, who was chief of medicine, set up a six-month special program for upgrading my medical knowledge, after which I began my surgical residency.

At the end of my second year at Walter Reed, I met Dr. Vince Pennisi, a plastic surgeon who had come to Walter Reed from St. Francis Memorial Hospital, which was a private hospital in San Francisco. After I performed several operations with him, he suggested that I go into plastic and reconstructive surgery. General Heaton wanted to send me to Fort Sam Houston, which was a great military hospital. The program in plastic surgery at Fort Sam Houston was good, but I told General Heaton that I really wanted to go to St. Francis, even though it was a civilian hospital. There were thirty applicants for the single annual residency at St. Francis, but I was the one selected and became the first military physician ever to complete a residency in a civilian hospital.

This was January 1957, and the residency did not begin until summer. For two months I worked at the Walter Reed Institute of Pathology, and then in March I was assigned to Camp Mercury, Nevada, where I measured radiation levels in animals exposed to atomic bomb tests.

I was at Camp Mercury for the detonation of two bombs, which was truly an awe-inspiring sight. The first one was suspended from the top of a 30-foot tower in the center of a long valley in a very pronounced bowl. In preparation, we staked out pigs at different distances and then retreated some five miles. We were told to face away from the blast to protect our eyes, but we wore no protective clothing because those in charge felt we would not be exposed to dangerous radiation at that distance. As a matter of fact, there were some troops in trenches only 2500 feet from the blast.

It was only a 20-megaton bomb, but after the explosion everything turned pure white. Then I felt a little heat on the back of my neck. When we were told it was all right to turn around, we could see the mushroom cloud rising from which emerged a small circle of dust. Faster and faster this cloud of dust moved toward us. Then, it went by us with a loud BANG! It broke windows in our nearby vehicles, all of which made it very clear to me that I never wanted to be in a war with atomic weapons.

I reported to St. Francis Memorial Hospital on July 1, 1957 for my residency training in plastic and hand surgery. There were two groups of plastic surgeons at St. Francis. One was headed by Dr. George Pierce and the other by Dr. Jerry O'Connor. Pierce approached plastic surgery one way and O'Connor another, but I learned from both. I was also fortunate to be trained in surgery of the hand by Dr. Sterling Bunnell, who, along with Dr. L. D. Howard, was the leading hand surgeon at the time.

We worked primarily on accident victims, but we also did some cosmetic work on important people. After I finished my two years at St. Francis, George Pierce made me feel very good about all my hard work by saying, "You've been the best resident we've had here."

In July 1959 I returned to Walter Reed as the Assistant Chief of Plastic Surgery, and two years later I became Chief of Plastic Surgery at Letterman General Hospital in San Francisco, where I remained until I retired from the U.S. Army on June 30, 1966.

Beginning in 1959, I also had the good fortune to be assigned on a temporary basis to the Surgical Recovery Team of the Man in Space Program. I served as the plastic and reconstructive member of the medical team in case there was trauma involved in the recovery process. I participated in Projects Mercury and Gemini, including John Glenn's first flight into space in 1962.

When I retired, I had over twenty years of service time. I had considered going for thirty years; in fact, Colonel Hal Jennings, who would soon become Surgeon General, encouraged me to do so. It was a very difficult decision, but family responsibilities convinced me it was time to leave the military and establish a private practice in Redding, California.

I decided on Redding because the nearest plastic surgeons were in Sacramento and Eugene, Oregon, and because of the natural beauty of the surrounding area. The day I arrived in Redding for my interview, the sky was azure blue, I could see snow-capped mountains in the distance, and the weather was 65 degrees. It was gorgeous. I thought to myself, this is the place, and I've been here ever since.

I want to reemphasize how fortunate I was to have performed a wide variety of plastic, reconstructive, and hand surgeries in topnotch army hospitals. These had included correcting congenital deformities and repairing severe injuries to the face and all parts of the body, treatment of burn wounds, and a wide spectrum of other bodily deformities. I must have worked on thousands of such cases, which well prepared me for my practice in Redding. In my first fifteen years in Redding I probably spent three to four nights a week in emergency rooms, often working most or all of the night operating on trauma victims.

There were also various selections of surgical problems that required reconstruction of deforming injuries, and these too contributed to a thoroughly challenging and satisfying practice in Redding. Patients came from as far away as Chico, which was 75 miles to the south, and once a month I went to a clinic in Alturas to work on people who could not afford to travel to Redding. When I retired from private practice in 1992, I had practiced medicine for twenty-one years in the Army and twenty-six years in Redding.

It was time to retire, but I was damned if I was going to spend my retirement years sitting around watching television. I turned my attention to growing roses on the back of our property and collecting and polishing fossil rocks from my many excursions to the Southwest. It took us five years and a lot of perspiration to build our rose garden. We had a worker help us carry in 220 railroad ties and countless wheelbarrows filled with good black dirt. At first we planted about 400 varieties of roses, but as we aged and the work became harder for us, we downsized to about half that number. We now have two wonderful helpers, and we still take great pleasure in the roses we grow, even exhibiting prize winners in our local and district rose societies.

I truly enjoyed collecting fossils and rocks. These excursions were often family affairs, as we traveled to remote areas of Nevada, Utah, Colorado, Arizona, and New Mexico searching for specimens. The entire process fascinated me. With help from a few excellent fossil and rock hunters, I studied enough geology and paleontology to understand what was happening. It is an indescribable feeling to find a specimen such as a dinosaur bone and realize that you are the first person to have touched it in more than 65 million years! My home is still filled fossil specimens from my collecting days.

Beginning in 1991, I also spent eleven years serving on the Veterans Administration's National Advisory Committee for Former Prisoners of War. My contribution was to educate the members on health problems former POWs were likely to suffer and what should be done about them. I found both support and resistance in the VA. The chairman of the committee was Dick Stratton. He was a marvelous person, who had been a POW in North Vietnam for more than six years.[1] He had been tortured by the North Vietnamese and was naturally very supportive of my recommendations.

I maintained that a great deal of the damage that had been done to the bodies of the former POWs was not always visible, even with lab tests and x-rays. Unfortunately, the men had to show symptoms before VA doctors acknowledged they did indeed have disabilities. When the good Lord made the human body, He produced a marvelous thing, with lots of physical reserves. However, the organs of former POWs had been so adversely affected because of severe malnutrition, vitamin deficiencies, beatings, and long exposure to bitterly cold weather that they had used up most of these precious reserves. There have been several articles in medical journals about concentration camp victims that describe the residual effects of their internment, and we experienced much the same kind of abuse. I accumulated and presented all the information I could find, and this contributed to the Veterans Administration's growing recognition of these long-term effects.

When I first came on the Advisory Committee, every VA hospital was autonomous and made its own decisions. We tried to standardize their handling of POW concerns. Most of the hospitals agreed to make this change, but some did not, which means that diagnoses and treatment could still vary in specific hospitals.

It was also a challenge to convince former POWs to go in for their protocol physicals. Initially, some of the doctors did not understand the protocol, but today most of them have been trained to look for certain things and to ask specific questions. Some claims are not really defensible, and some men have learned how to play the system, but most claims are valid.

I served on the Advisory Committee for eleven years before I finally resigned because I believed fresh blood was needed. When I joined the committee, I was the only doctor. Today, there are several, and things seem to be going better.

---

1.   Navy pilot Lt. Commander Richard Stratton was shot down in 1967 over North Vietnam. After being severely tortured, he was forced to bow to his captors before international television cameras. A documentary about his captivity, titled *2251 Days*, aired in 1974. See also, Scott Blakey, *Prisoner of War: The Survival of Commander Richard A. Stratton* (Norwell, MA: Anchor Press, 1978).

◆   ◆   ◆

When I view the entirety of my life, I can certainly point to segments that were painful and even life-threatening, but there is so much for which I am grateful. People tell me what a bad break is was to have been a prisoner of war for almost three years and then to suffer the dark cloud of suspicion that hovered over all of us after we returned home. But from the bad can come good. I have experienced a very rewarding medical career, and I have gathered a number of wonderful friends. Some have become like brothers to me, and others were instrumental in helping me advance professionally. I also have learned a great deal about human nature and how to judge the character of a man. Above all, I have gained an abiding appreciation and understanding of freedom.

The good began with my parents and siblings, who did so much to help me establish a foundation of faith on which to base my life. They taught me to work hard, live honestly, and to interact with my fellow human beings without doing harm to anyone.

My teachers, from K-12 through my undergraduate and postgraduate studies and beyond, also greatly enriched my life. So many physicians, and especially surgeons, willingly shared their knowledge and skills. They not only taught me how the body functions but also how to help and understand those in need.

It was my privilege to have served under several extraordinary officers, especially Surgeon General Leonard Heaton and Colonel Hal Jennings. General Heaton was responsible for my being admitted to arguably the best surgical residencies in the country, and Colonel Jennings was my immediate commander at Walter Reed. There is no way I could have paid for my medical training, so I am deeply indebted to the U.S. Army itself. Every day of my training as a physician was paid for and performed under the auspices of the U.S. Army. Premedical schooling came during my World War II service, and I was able to continue my medical studies after the war under the GI Bill.

My patients have always meant a lot to me. When in retirement I am asked if I miss the practice of surgery, I always respond, "No, not that much, but I really do miss the friendship of my patients."

I am deeply grateful to my immediate family for tolerating me during the hard times we endured after I returned from Korea. All former POWs were strict fathers, more so than we should have been, but my children put up with me, and thank God they are now also my friends. I am so proud of them all and what they have done with their lives. My oldest son Will is a very successful university professor and clinical psychologist, specializing in statistical methodology. He currently teaches at University of California, Merced. He has written eleven books and is nationally and internationally known for his work. He lives in the Sierra foothills with his darling wife Cindy.

My daughter Margaret is a teacher in the Redding area. She is married to an attorney, Manuel Garcia, and they have two bright and beautiful children, Jennifer and Manuel, Jr., both currently students. We are so proud of them.

My son Bryan is a computer expert who is married to a lovely Chinese lady, Emily. They live in the Bay Area of California with their brilliant children, Katy and Matthew, who every day continue to impress us with their studies and abilities. We see a bright future for them, and they are truly precious.

My son Mark, equally as bright as his siblings, unfortunately died too young of a cardiac condition. He death was one of the most difficult events in our lives to accept. We miss him sorely. He has two sons: Kevin William, studying to be a chef, and Thomas, who resides in Redding with his mother, Denise.

The children Karen brought into our marriage include Todd Kamla, the oldest. He lives with his sweet wife, Jackie, in nearby Mt. Shasta, and is a distributor for a retail company. His two wonderful children, son Chase and daughter Taylor, are excellent young students who also have many athletic and artistic talents.

Karen's son Zach Kamla, who served in the Marine Corps for four years, works as a substance abuse counselor in Redding. He has steadfastly cared for us with love and support, especially during my illnesses and surgeries during these past few years.

Our youngest, Dana Post, is a teacher and resides with her family in Bremerton, Washington. Her husband Nathan is a firefighter lieutenant and they have two adorable young sons, Garrett and Aidan, the youngest (and liveliest) of our grandchildren.

I feel so blessed by this wonderful family. Who could ask for anything more?

Adequate words fail me when acknowledging the contributions of my remarkable wife Karen, who gently and faithfully loved me through my healing from PTSD. She always stood ready to give me comfort, encouragement, and sage advice. What would I have done without her? Like the wives of all former POWs, Karen would be the first to admit that we POWs had problems and were not easy to live with, but these magnificent women have stuck with us when we needed them the most.

My final and greatest thanks go to my Lord, who saw to it that I received all these blessings and who was always there to help me survive that hell hole in North Korea when so many others did not. Even in my darkest hours, my faith in

Him was unwavering. Indeed, he set us prisoners free! How can I thank Him enough?

Lew Carlson (left) and Bill Shadish at the Shadish home in Redding, California.

Bill and Karen Shadish in their rose garden

◆　　　◆　　　◆

This story must end with some comments on that most precious of all American possessions, freedom. Is freedom the ability to say anything one wishes without restraint or other considerations? Not likely. Freedom includes responsibilities. We have all heard the phrase freedom is not free, but it bears repeating. Freedom has been paid for in blood, sweat, and lives since this country began.

We have witnessed how tyrants have historically attempted to spread their dictatorships to other countries: Hitler, Stalin, Lenin and more recently the leaders in China, Iraq, Iran, Syria, and North Korea. Freedom has to be fought for and guarded diligently and sincerely by the people of this nation and any other nation that wishes to be free. Let there be no mistake. There will always be evil leaders in this world. Go back through history and see what has happened time after time after time. It seems when one evil disappears another quickly fills in the gap. Evil leaders all have one thing in common. They do not, cannot, tolerate freedom. They must obliterate it or they cannot continue their wanton destruction and domination. Even when we rid ourselves of our present enemies and dictators, new ones will spring up, just as they are now across the globe. We will always have to fight for freedom; we must fight for it; we cannot sit back and relax and we cannot give in.

In our world, there are givers and there are takers. Soldiers and veterans are givers. They have left families and put themselves in harm's way to protect our freedom. So when I think of freedom, I especially think of these men and women. I do not want to see my family live without freedom, and I know we have freedom for all because so many of our bravest citizens have served and died for our country.

Freedom is a wonderful thing, but one cannot really understand what it means until it is lost, and I mean totally lost. Once lost, there is nothing sweeter than freedom itself. Imagine being unable to say or do any of the things you would ordinarily do with impunity. Without freedom, you cannot travel, choose your work, or where you live. You have no choice in selecting your leaders. Even something as insignificant as deciding what you will do tomorrow can lead to the threat of imprisonment or death. No one understands this better than former POWs. I can assure you, if our families were to be threatened by the yoke of tyranny, it would be over our dead bodies.

Unfortunately, one cannot describe freedom sufficiently to those who have never lost it. It is too often taken for granted by those who enjoy it but do little or nothing to preserve it. Freedom demands great responsibilities. We must understand that our neighbors have freedom, as do others with whom we disagree, and they guard their freedom as jealously as we do our own. This does not mean that one can go off the deep end and make scurrilous remarks or commit actions that might incite violence. We may disagree openly with each other, if we do so honestly, but there is a limit to honest disagreement that does not include abusive remarks about our leaders and our troops.

When we POWs returned from Korea, we were not treated well by some in this country. We were all considered collaborators and treated as such before the overwhelming majority of us were finally cleared of all such charges. Eleven men were convicted of collaborating with the enemy, and in their instances the punishments were justified. However, as I look at the political scene today, I wonder what the punishment should be for those politicians who stoop to such low levels in attempting to gain political advantage by blaspheming our President and our military, forgetting the needs of our country and the war we are fighting against terrorism.

I clearly remember that while in prison camp, few if any men voiced enmity toward President Truman. He was our president, and Republican or Democrat, we stood behind him under punishment and threat of death. When our nation is at war, we must put aside our differences and unite behind our government. Doing otherwise helps only the enemy and insults those who are fighting for our freedom. If change is needed, the ballot box is where it should be done. Meanwhile, let's all say, "God Bless You" to those doing the fighting for us.

APPENDIX

WILLIAM R. SHADISH TIME LINE

May 16, 1924	- Birth of William R. Shadish in Bridgeville, Pennsylvania
June 1942	- Graduates from Bridgeville's Lincoln High School
June 1942	- Takes a job as machinist for Carnegie Steel Company
February 13, 1943	- Joins the U. S. Army and takes basic training at Camp Swift, Texas
May 1943	- Studies engineering in the Army's Specialized Training Program at Carnegie Tech in Pittsburgh
February 1944	- Assigned to take pre-med courses at Syracuse University
September 1945	- Begins medical studies at Long Island College of Medicine
March 19, 1946	- Honorably discharged from the U.S. Army for the first time
January 1946—June 1949	- Using the GI Bill, completes medical studies at Long Island College of Medicine
June 22, 1949	- Re-enlists in the U. S. Army
July 1949—June 1950	- Serves internship at Kaiser's Permanente Hospital in Oakland, California.
July 2, 1950	- Flies from Travis Air Force Base to assignment in Kyoto, Japan
August 7, 1950	- Flies to Pusan, South Korea
August 7—Nov. 30, 1950	- Combat physician with the 2nd Battalion Medical Aid Station of the Ninth Regiment of the Second Division
December 1, 1950	- Taken Prisoner of War at Kunu-ri
December 4–25, 1950	- Marched through the mountains of North Korea
December 25, 1950—	- Arrives in Death Valley
January 22, 1951	- The majority of American prisoners leave Death Valley for Camp 5, but Shadish remains behind with the remaining 300, only 106 of whom will survive.

March 12, 1951	- The 106 survivors leave Death Valley for a seven-day march to Camp 5; only 94 will make it.
March 19, 1951	- The 94 survivors of Death Valley arrive in Camp 5
March 19—July 19, 1951	- Served as physician to the Enlisted Men's Compound in Camp 5
July 19, 1951	- Moved to Officers' Compound in Camp 5 and no longer allowed to administer to the medical needs of the Enlisted Men
October 22, 1951	- Transferred from Camp 5 to Camp 2
September 5, 1953	- Liberation
September 6–7, 1953	- Freedom Village and nearby hospital
September 7–18, 1953	- Tokyo Army Hospital
September 20, 1953	- Lands in San Francisco
Sept. 21–Dec. 31, 1953	- St. Alban's Naval Hospital (including a 90-day convalescence leave)
January 1954—July, 1957	- Residency training at Walter Reed Army Hospital to become a surgeon
February—July 1957	- Surgeon, Atomic Energy Project, Camp Mercury, Nevada
July 1957—June 1959	- Residency training in plastic and hand surgery, St. Francis Memorial Hospital, San Francisco
July 1959–1962	- Assistant Chief of Plastic Surgery, Walter Reed Army Hospital, Washington, D.C.
1962–1966	- Chief of Plastic Surgery, Letterman General Hospital, San Francisco
1959–1966	- Served on the Surgical Recovery Teams of the Man in Space Program's Mercury and Gemini Projects. In 1962, assigned to NASA and John Glenn's first flight into space.
June 30, 1966	- Retires from U.S. Army
July 1, 1966—Nov. 1, 1992	- Private practice in Redding, CA, as specialist in plastic and reconstruction surgery and surgery of the hand

1969–1994	- Served as a Member of the Northern California Emergency Care Council
1984–1986	- Served as Surgical Consultant to the Department of Veterans Affairs Clinic in Redding, California
1988–1989	- Served as a Gubernatorial Appointee to the California Board of Medical Quality Assurance
1989–2000	- Served on the Veterans Administration's National Advisory Committee for Former Prisoners of War, Washington, D.C.
October 2003	- Appointed to the California Veterans Administration Board
1992—Present	- Retired to work in Rose Garden and as an amateur paleontologist

MEDICAL EXPERIENCES IN COMMUNIST POW CAMPS IN KOREA. A REPORT READ BY MAJOR CLARENCE L. ANDERSON, MAJOR ALEXANDER M. BOYSEN, CAPTAIN SIDNEY ESENSTEN, CAPTAIN GENE N. LAM, AND CAPTAIN WILLIAM R. SHADISH TO THE SECTION ON MILITARY MEDICINE AT THE 103RD ANNUAL MEETING OF THE AMERICAN MEDICAL ASSOCIATION, SAN FRANCISCO, JUNE 24, 1954.[1]

The following report constitutes a general recital of the experiences and observations of five American medical officers who were prisoners of war of the Communists in Korea. No attempt has been made to present this material as a scientific study. The period of observation started in July 1950, and continued until September 1953, when the last group of prisoners of war was repatriated. A large part of the accumulated prisoner of war experience is included. Some of the smaller groups, composed of men who were captured after Jan. 1, 1952, were not observed directly by any of the captured medical officers.

THREE PHASES OF CAPTIVITY

The entire period of captivity is divided into three general time phases. The first phase started with capture and ended with arrival in the first permanent camp. It was characterized by lack of food and shelter, forced marches, and exposure to the elements. Men were forced to march through snow storms without adequate clothing or food covering. Food was supplied and prepared by the local inhabitants. Frequently there was no food for 24 to 72 hour periods. The only water

---

1.   This presentation subsequently appeared in the September 11, 1954 issue of the *Journal of the American Medical Association*.

available for drinking was snow or water from polluted sources, such as standing wells, creeks, and rice paddies. With few exceptions, the prisoners got to rear areas by marching and carrying the wounded, either on improvised litters or on their backs. Injuries resulting from prolonged marches and exposure to cold were common. Dysentery made its first appearance. Medical supplies were nonexistent, and treatment was limited entirely to first aid, using improvised splints and rag dressings. Most of the prisoners experienced severe mental depression.

The second phase began with the arrival at the first permanent camp and ended about October 1951, when the first beneficial effects of the armistice negotiations were felt. This was a phase of profound deprivation of all the necessities of life. The diet was grossly inadequate. The 1950 Thanksgiving meal of one group of 500 men furnishes a typical example. Each man received a millet ball weighing less than 200 grams, and the whole group was given soup prepared by boiling nine heads of cabbage in water. Group sanitation and personal hygiene were at their lowest levels. The men were housed in small, unheated overcrowded vermin-infested Korean farm houses. No clothing was issued until July 1951. Medicine and medical care were inadequate, and morale reached its lowest ebb. In the face of all these conditions, sickness and death became the order of the day.

The third phase began in October 1951, with gradually increasing quantities of food, clothing, and medicine. This period was characterized by many fluctuations in the attitude of the captors toward the prisoners, which appeared to follow changes in the political situation and the armistice conference. The diet remained inadequate in protein and vitamin content. Housing was gradually improved to a point of relative comfort, and clothing was sufficient for survival. Sanitary conditions, while never good, underwent a gradual improvement. Medical care never became adequate. Avitaminoses were prevalent.

MEDICAL CARE

The health of all United Nations' prisoners was neglected throughout the period of captivity. Before the onset of armistice negotiations the Communists showed no uniform desire to keep the prisoners alive. By the spring of 1951 the food shortage had become so acute that weeds growing adjacent to the prison compound were boiled and eaten. Most of the serious disease epidemics occurred during the first year of captivity. Pneumonia and dysentery were epidemic at this time. Some of the captured medical officers were allowed to see patients. Medical and surgical supplies, however, were doled out on a day-to-day basis. The so-called hospital compounds were frequently the coldest buildings in the camp. The patients slept and lived on the floors of these filthy, crowded compounds. It was common for them to awaken in the morning and find that the man sleeping on either side had died during the night. No provision was made for the prisoners to be properly clothed, and their diet was always poor. At times they were put on a special diet consisting of an unseasoned preparation of soupy rice.

Penicillin and the sulfonamides were available sporadically and in such small quantities that it was not possible to treat all who needed these drugs. On one occasion we were given two million units of aqueous penicillin for the treatment of approximately 100 cases of pneumonia. Our captors refused to allow more than six grams of sufonamide for the treatment of any single pneumonia patient. Frequently, the only medicaments available were cough tablets for pneumonia and charcoal tablets for dysentery. Surgical problems were handled in an equally haphazard manner. It was necessary to wait several weeks to obtain a few surgical instruments and the barest minimum of anesthetic materials. Incision and drainage of abscesses were usually carried out without anesthesia by using improvised instruments, such as a knife made from the arch of a combat boot.

Deaths—Virtually all of the deaths in the Communist prisoner of war camps were caused directly or indirectly by starvation, exposure, and the harassment by the enemy. The lack of medicaments was not the most important factor. During the first month or two of captivity most of the deaths occurred among the wounded. During the succeeding three to five months most of the men died either from pneumonia or dysentery, or from a combination of these two. After the first five or six months of captivity the majority of deaths occurred among persons suffering from pellagra or beriberi. During one five-month period there were between five and 28 deaths per day in one camp in North Korea. None of these men had illnesses that would have caused death had they been under normal conditions.

After October 1951, the prisoners were put on a subsistence diet and were given sufficient clothing and reasonably warm housing. All of the men continued to suffer from periodic loss of day and night vision, and bleeding from sourness of the mouth and lips. There were occasional cases of pneumonia and dysentery. Sickness and death became so common during the first year and a half of captivity that the prisoners began to feel that any sickness would be fatal. In an attempt to overcome this attitude, the captured physicians coined a very unfortunate term, "give-up-itis." The use of this term had its desired immediate effect on the prisoners. It made them realize that the individual's fighting spirit had to be maintained at a high level for him to survive any illness. The term, "give-up-itis," has recently gotten wide circulation in the public press. The erroneous impression has been created that prisoners of war who were in good physical health gave up and died; this is not true. Every prisoner of war in Korea who died had suffered from malnutrition, exposure to cold, and continued harassment by the Communists. Contributing causes to the majority of deaths were prolonged cases of respiratory infection and diarrhea. Under such conditions, it is amazing, not that there was a high death rate, but that there was a reasonably good rate of survival.

Chinese Physicians—During the summer and fall of 1951, all of the British and American doctors were gradually replaced by Chinese. Most of the Chinese doctors exhibited a wide range of medical incompetence. Most of them had a maximum of six months formal schooling, and we saw only one physician who appeared to be well trained. The Chinese doctor who was put in the most responsible position was one who was best oriented politically. The average Chinese doctor who conducted sick call in the prisoner of war camps elicited only the chief complaint and prescribed medicine for symptomatic relief. It was a general rule that only one symptom would be treated at a time; therefore, if a patient suffered from nigh blindness and diarrhea, it was necessary for him to decide which of these complaints was bothering him more before he went on sick call. He would not be treated for both conditions.

The Communists introduced us to several unusual types of medical treatment. One Chinese doctor used a series of short needles attached to spring vibrators for the treatment of pain. The needles were placed in the skin around the painful area and then were made to vibrate. As one might suspect, some cases of back pain and headache were cured by this treatment. At one time a Chinese doctor decided that all of our visual disturbances were caused by glaucoma. He injected hypertonic sodium chloride solution subconjunctivally. Another notable treatment was used for avitaminosis. Bile was obtained from the gallbladders of pigs when they were butchered, and it was then dispensed to all who complained of vitamin deficiency diseases. This treatment had its desired effect in keeping patients away from sick call. In the summer of 1951 a great Russian panacea was used in treating 56 seriously ill patients. This consisted of the subcutaneous transplant of small pieces of chicken liver that had been incubated in a weak solution of penicillin. These patients were immediately put on an attractive, high calory, high protein, high vitamin diet. In all cases, the chicken liver either sloughed through the operative site or became a hard, tender nodule. None of these men died, and we were thus allowed to witness another miracle of Soviet science.

INDOCTRINATION

The most important single consideration that placed the prisoners of war in North Korea apart from any other group of American prisoners of war was Communist indoctrination. This indoctrination had a profound effect on the general health of the group. The medical profession and the American people as a whole have a great deal to learn from a study of the techniques, purposes, and effectiveness of Communist indoctrination as it was used on Americans in North Korea. There is no reason to believe that the Communist indoctrination techniques that were used on the prisoners of war were different in any way from the general pattern of indoctrination that is being used in Communist-dominated countries today. It is important to realize that every aspect of the daily life of the prisoner, from the moment of capture to the time of release, was part of the general plan of indoctrination. At the time of capture, each prisoner was given the general theme of indoctrination: "We are your friends. Your conditions of living are bad now, but we will work together to improve them. We will correct the errors in your thinking. Once you have learned the truth, we will send you back to your families."

Steps in Indoctrination—The first necessary step was to break down the normal resistence to an alien ideology. This was accomplished by keeping the prisoners cold, hungry, and in a state of disorganized confusion until each person realized that resistance meant starvation and death. It was emphasized repeatedly that the prisoners were no longer members of the armed forces of their nation, and all attempts to maintain a military organization were harshly punished. The planners of this indoctrination program did not condone the shooting of large numbers of prisoners. Instead, they resorted to starvation and exposure to cold. After a few months of this treatment the resistance of the survivors had softened. The second phase of indoctrination consisted of an intensive formal study program. For a period of approximately one year, most of the waking hours of the prisoners were spent in some form of supervised study. Food was gradually improved and more clothing was issued. It was made painfully clear to each prisoner that living conditions would be improved only so long as there was no resistance to the study program. The formal study program consisted of an endless repetition of two main themes: first, that the United States government is imperialistic, run by and for the wealthy few, and, second, that Communism reflects the aims and desires of all the people and is the only true democracy. The main propaganda technique that was used was ceaseless repetition of the main theme.

During the third phase all formal studies were stopped. The groundwork had been laid, and, to a large extent, the purposes of the indoctrination program had been fulfilled. Books, pamphlets, and newspapers became available in quantity. During this time, the Chinese conducted many individual and small group interviews. They attempted to find points of individual susceptibility on such grounds as race, religion, or economic status. The most intensive subject for special indoctrination was the bacteriological warfare hoax. Throughout the period of captivity there were many instances of individual brutality. Solitary confinement, beatings, withholding food and water, and exposure to cold were common punishments. Resistance leaders were taken away from the main body of prisoners and kept either in solitary confinement or in small groups of recalcitrants. No one escaped the indoctrination program. When a captured medical officer stated that he had no interest in politics, he was told, "Up to this time your education has been incomplete. You have only learned how to cure. We Communists will teach you whom to cure."

Purposes—The indoctrination program had a two-fold purpose: first, the selection and conversion of susceptible persons, and, second, group neutralization. During the first year of captivity there was a continual regrouping of prisoners in an attempt to isolate resistance groups. They were separated according to rank and later according to national and racial groups. There were a few persons who eventually accepted the Communist ideology, but they constituted only a small minority of any single group. The second purpose of indoctrination, group neutralization, was far more important and somewhat more successful. The Communists fostered discontent and distrust within the groups. So long as there was no unity of purpose, there could be no effective resistance.

COMMENT

The experiences of this group, therefore, form a valuable basis for the understanding of Communist aims and techniques. Most persons in the United States are probably guilty of a certain smugness about the possibility of Communism actually taking over our country. It is worthwhile to keep in mind two well-known facts: first, no country has ever been taken over by Communists because the majority of the people in that country wanted it; second, no country once it has been taken over by Communism has ever reverted to another form of government. Communist tyranny has been maintained by the application of indoctrination techniques similar in every respect to those that were practiced on the prisoners of war in North Korea. A relatively small group of Communists with a definite plan would have little difficulty in wresting power from a government that is paralyzed by a coalition of small groups concentrating on their own short-sighted interests.

The people of the United States must realize that the spread of Communism anywhere in the world, whether by armed aggression on by internal infiltration, constitutes a direct threat to our survival as a nation. Americans must work against Communism by being vigilant; they must work for democracy by constantly striving toward the democratic ideal of an enlightened people participating in their government. Physicians have an influence that is out of proportion to their numbers. That influence should be used to fight Communism by intelligently promoting democracy.

DISEASES DIAGNOSED IN HOFONG (DEATH VALLEY) AND PYŎKTONG (CAMP 5), AS REPORTED BY DR. WILLIAM SHADISH TO U.S. ARMY MEDICAL AUTHORITIES ON JANUARY 14–15, 1954, FOUR MONTHS AFTER HIS LIBERATION

Phase 1—DISEASES SEEN IN HOFONG (DEATH VALLEY), DECEMBER 25, 1950—MARCH 12, 1951:

After the Chinese marched the majority of the prisoners out of Death Valley to Camp 5 at Pyŏktong on January 22, 1951, Dr. Gene Lam, Dr. Edwin Ecklund, Dr. Peter Kubinek, Dr. Burt Coers, and I and approximately 20 medical corpsmen were left to care for 250-300 of the more seriously sick and wounded men, who, due to their inability to survive a long march at that time, were left behind by orders of the Chinese C.O. after much insistence by us.... In this phase the death rate increased, one day (January 24, 1951) reaching a rate of 14 deaths. Of course, at this time, morale was at its lowest. Diseases seen in this phase were:

(A) **Dysentery**—100 percent of the camp were afflicted at one time or another, with usually 25-35 percent of the camp affected severely at times.

(B) **Severe Malnutrition**—as evidenced by weight loss—100 percent of the men

© **Cold Injury**—practically 100 percent of the men. Approximately 10-15 percent with tissue loss

(D) **Infectious Hepatitis**—one epidemic in Hofong—20-30 cases; approximately 50 percent died

(E) Labor Pneumonia—approximately 100 cases; of this group only a few known survivors. The pneumonia cases were classified into three categories for therapeutic reasons:

1. Gross bilateral consolidation—in a toxic state

2. Unilateral consolidation

3. No group consolidation, but definite auscultatory signs of possible early pneumonia

For therapy we had only sulfadiazine tablets, 0.5 gm., enough to give only a few selected cases a <u>minimum</u> effective dose daily for about 5 days. This entailed selecting those few who were probably too seriously ill to recover spontaneously, yet not so far advanced as to assure that we were giving such valuable, life saving, but scarce, drug to a hopeless cause while there were others who could be saved.

Those who were in the early stages of Category 2 above fell into this classification nicely. However, many in Category 1 were so grossly consolidated and so toxic that it was evident that the small amount of sulfadiazine available for them would probably be used fruitlessly. On the other hand, in those cases where a positive diagnosis was not possible, we again attempted to withhold the drug. As soon a definite early signs of pneumonia appeared in the Category 3 type of patient, he would receive sulfadiazine, if available, for his chances for recovery were best then. The dosage was 1 gram sulfadiazine by mouth, every six hours for 3 to 5 days. Even with this selection, the small amount of drug available made treatment very limited and the mortality of all cases, treated and untreated, was over 90 percent. The untreated cases suffered a mortality rate of practically 100 percent while among the treated cases only about 40 percent died.

We had always to combat the efforts of the Chinese Communists who wanted each man to get an equal share and tried to insist that we give each man one tablet of sulfadiazine per day. We did manage to win our way in this.

Phase 2—DISEASES SEEN IN PYÖKTONG (CAMP 5), MARCH 19, 1951—JULY 19, 1951:

I saw the same diseases in Camp 5 as were observed in Hofong (Death Valley), with the additions of the dietary deficiency diseases, which all became grossly evident during this period. In fact, with the advance of summer, pneumonia dwindled to practically a nonentity, while as time progressed the dietary deficience diseases became more and more pronounced. Following are enumerated the diseases most commonly seen in Camp 5:

(A) Dysentery—This was usually seen as an acute type of illness, explosive in onset, often with fever, watery BMs up to 50/day, and prostration which subsided, but not completely, so that there remained a chronic type of loose stool, 3-20/day, with blood and mucous, clearing for several weeks, only to begin again, but this time not so violently. In this chronic phase there was less of the prostration but more severe cramping. It appeared to have been a mixture of bacillary and amoebic dysentery.

These men were treated with appropriate sulfa tablets, when available, 0.5 gm tablets, 6-8/24 hours for 48-72 hours. If sulfa was unobtainable, we gave the patient charcoal tablets 0.5 gm, 2/day. Fluids were forced.

Meals containing soy beans often raised the incidence of diarrhea in the compounds.

At least 50-75 percent of the prisoners at Pyŏktong had diarrhea of one cause or another during this period, <u>simultaneously</u>, throughout this period.

(B) F. U. O.—A great incidence of febrile diseases appeared in April and May of 1951. The fever spiked, often to 104-105 degrees F., but irregularly. The fever often became sustained for 3-4 days, then returned either to normal or a spiking pattern again. There were usually no positive physical finding other than an elevated temperature, and often the only symptoms were headache and malaise. Practically all cases subsided spontaneously in from 6-12 days, with only a few recurrences. A few appeared to be malaria (typical). Incidentally, we found few breeding spots of Anopheles mosquitoes around our compound, but there were many mosquitoes present. An attempt was made to destroy all breeding places in our area.

Chinese often gave these patients Atabrine, 2 Tabs/day with no effect in most cases. Two aspirin tabs 0.5 gm often reduced fever temporarily, but not always.

(C) Bronchitis—Very prevalent in the early spring of 1951. Usual complaint was a persistent, dry cough. Physical exam showed nothing but coarse bronchial rales over the entire chest. A Japanese(?) medication in tablet form, called Neo-Hustin, was effective as cough suppressant when allowed to dissolve in the mouth.

One thing that perpetuated the bronchitis was the smoking of the harsh Korean tobacco, the only tobacco available at this time. When a patient suffering from bronchitis stopped smoking, he usually improved. We found that in the experience of most of our patients the only way to stop smoking was to do it abruptly. Tapering off often did not work.

(D) Mouth Lesions—In about May 1951 (approx. 4-5 months after the beginning of the poor diet) many began to complain of "sore mouth and tongue," especially while smoking or eating hot foods. Eventually all the men experienced this, with the symptoms clearing spontaneously in one or two weeks, only to recur after a month or two. It also appeared that the symptoms lasted longer at each recurrence. Physical exam would reveal cheilosis, a reddened, cracked tongue, and tender gingival areas. As could be expected we later found that Vitamin B2, when available, could cure this in 4-5 days.

There were also cases of swollen, bleeding, extremely tender gums that made eating difficult. In these cases there were often no cheilosis or glossitis. Although only the minor part of these were full-blown cases of scurvy, all prisoners were suffering from this disease to some degree or other.

Now when individuals such as prisoners of war, suffering from both Vitamin B2 and C deficiency diseases simultaneously, as many did, contracted an infectious process in his oral cavity, one can expect extensive lesions. This happened in Pyöktong in late May 1951, when there occurred an epidemic of oral lesions that appeared pyrogenic in origin, superimposed upon a B2 and C deficiency condition. As a result all were resistant to cure and approx. 10-15 percent of these cases progressed to deep ulcerative lesions of the gingival and buccal areas, especially at points making contact with teeth edges. Some of the ulcerations were deep almost to the point of complete penetration of the buccal areas. The men lost weight, for they found eating almost impossible.

At first only Potassium Permanganate (KMNO4) was available. This was used in a solution of approx. 1:1000C strength. However, after much insistence to the Chinese, some Vit. B2 and Vit. C tablets arrived. I found that 2 Tabs of each/day, along with the KMNO4 mouthwash, cleared the majority of cases, although a few required higher doses. Only one man succumbed to a generalized oral infection that became completely unassailable.

The spread of this disease was difficult to control. One habit which may have aided the dissemination of the infection was that of "passing around the precious cigarette butt." This I discouraged at every possible opportunity.

(E) Neuritic Pains—Almost every prisoner experienced the neuritic type, searing, shooting pain, deep in the thighs, commonly referred to by the men as "bone aches." They just became apparent in late March 1951. These pains were very severe, but curiously, occurred only at night. Arising and walking about relieved the pain to some extent. The malady started mildly, became progressively more severe, attained the peak at about 10-14 days after onset, and then slowly receded, spontaneously, terminating in complete permanent relief at about 18 days after onset. There seemed to be no residual damage. Recurrences were rare.

(F) Nutritional Edema—Soon after these attacks of neuritic pains, approx. 10 percent developed nutritional edema. This edema was dependent in nature, beginning in the ankles and progressing upwards to a maximum in about 10-14 days. Then the edema subsided, slowly and spontaneously, to a 1+ or 2+ edema of the ankles alone. At its worst, the edema was so acute that the skin was actually split by the forced stretching caused by the massive fluid collected.

(Of all these cases (roughly 200), a few were actually full-blown beriberi, with enlarged heart, systolic murmur, precordial pain, and generalized 4+ edema. The mortality was limited almost exclusively to these cases.)

Approximately 30-40 percent of these cases progressed to massive edema, including edema of the thighs, scrotum and penis. Little mental change was noted. The appetite remained normal in these patients. The most effective treatment was an improved diet and vitamin and protein therapy. For this reason I attempted to get the severe edema cases into sick company.

(G) Pellagra—From April to July I observed approximately 100 cases of pellagra, many of which were severe and resulted in death. These patients exhibited a reddened, thickened, cracked skin on the dorsum of the hands, feet, and on the exposed part of the chest. These areas often produced large vesicate lesions sometimes 6-7 cm in diameter, filled with a clear or straw-colored fluid. In pellagra we saw the 3 Ds: diarrhea, dermatitis, and dementia. The dementia caused apathy. This is what was termed (for lack of better words) "give-up-itis," or "face-to-the-wall syndrome." It was not "give-up-itis." These terribly sick men, who had lost at least half of their body weight, no longer cared about anything, refused to eat or exercise and simply turned their faces to the wall and died. They did not die because they gave up; they died because the had severe pellagra with its attendant severe apathy.

The only treatment available was a boric acid salve for use locally on the lesions, charcoal for the diarrhea, attempts to obtain better food (tried to get these men admitted to sick call, also) and <u>constant</u> prodding to keep the patient up and about.

(H) <u>Night Blindness</u>—Beginning about early April, a great number of men developed marked nocturnal loss of visual, most acutely in the center of the visual fields. Vit. A, when available, cured these cases easily in one or two days treatment.

(I) <u>Scabies</u>—Seen very often in early 1951, it is a highly contagious disease. It has a reddened scaling eruption that occurs in epidemic form in physically debilitated patients who are crowded inhabitants. It is caused by female mites burrowing into the skin and creating small, threadlike tunnels into which they lay their eggs. The sores that emerged on the skin cause intense itching.

(J) <u>Tuberculosis</u>—I can recall 20-25 cases of tuberculosis in Pyöktang during this period that could be <u>positively</u> diagnosed clinically. (There were <u>no</u> laboratory procedures available to us of <u>any</u> type). Most of these men died, including two of our physicians. The presenting symptoms usually were chest pain, cough and/or hemoptysis. The men would often complain of shortness of breath. When this happened we frequently found pleural effusion. I know of 4 men with positive evidence of Koch's infection in early 1951 that survived to repatriation. One had massive unilateral hydrothorax that cleared spontaneously over a period of 6 months, leaving only a pleural thickening and adhesives at the base of the affected lung.

(K) <u>Dental Disease</u>—The vitamin deficiency diseases were acute and for this reason the mouths were sore. The men could not brush their teeth for long periods of time. There were no toothbrushes, toothpaste, or soap available. Also, the grain foods contained small rocks that, when bit upon, caused fillings to be dislodged and teeth to break. Consequently many caries developed, as did peri-apical abscesses. No Chinese dental personnel were available, and only one small pair of forceps were present, about 4-5 inches in length. I did not attempt to do extracting until recurrent peri-apical abscesses began to prevent the afflicted man from eating. In the poor nutritional conditions the men suffered at this time, 4-5 days without food can be fatal. Therefore, I decided to extract selected cases.

At first no local anesthetic was available, so I attempted extraction without anesthesia. However, this was too hard on the patient, so I used a pre-extraction I. V. injection of 1/8-1/6 gr. morphine sulphate given slowly to achieve the necessary analgesia. This served the purpose beautifully. Later procaine became available. I used a procedure of nerve block and local infiltration. Between 50-75 extractions were done using these methods during this period.

(L) **Round Worm Disease (Ascaris Lumbricoides)**—These are worms that can grow to be a foot long. They are about 1/4 of an inch think, yellowish and firm in body. Their eggs are ingested in contaminated areas such as found in Korea. They mature in the intestine, migrate through the intestinal wall and enter the lymphatic system. They develop eventually in the lungs.

Mature forms migrate up the trachea and are often coughed out. One would see a man come running up, complaining, with the long yellow worm protruding from his nose. These can cause difficulty absorbing food and can even in some cases block the intestines causing complete impactions.

Additional Comments: One subject that should be breached before leaving this section is the Black Market procedures that prevailed in the Hofong and Pyöktong Camps. Men would appropriate the food rations and sell them to individuals. The valuables of the dead and dying men would be stolen and traded to the Koreans for tobacco. Cigarettes rolled with this tobacco would then sell for anywhere from $5—$20 each. Clothing (often stolen) would sell at outrageous prices. A few more procured medicine from sources unknown to myself and the other physicians and sold it to men dying for need of it at absurd prices. One could not track down these culprits, for the victim who had to pay the price would not reveal the source, for if he did he knew the source would be eliminated. This is one of the most deplorable things that happened among the U. N. prisoners of war in the hands of the Communists. The Turkish soldiers, incidentally, were active in such dealings.

After I was transferred to the officers compound in Pyöktong on July 19, 1951, I was relieved of all duties as a physician. In addition I was warned, as were the other physicians, that I was not to practice medicine in <u>any</u> form whatsoever, nor was I to "obstruct or undermine the work of the Chinese medical staff in the future." From this time forward I was in the same position as any other prisoner.

Dr. William Paul Skelton, III, who is a Professor of Medicine in the University of South Florida's College of Medicine, has written one of the best summarizations of the illnesses of the American POW. Dr. Skelton has also served as the POW Physician Coordinator at the James A. Haley Veterans Administration Medical

Center in Tampa, Florida. His treatise on the American exPOW has gone through multiple editions and is the most informative discussion of POW illnesses. He is to be commended for the tremendous work he has done on the subject.

Alice Stratton, the wife of a long-term POW in Vietnam, has produced an excellent discussion of the effects of prolonged separation on the military families of POWs. Her article can be found in the U.S. Naval Institute Proceedings of July 1978.

Another excellent reference book for understanding the relationships of former POWs to their families is Guy J. Kelnhofer's *Understanding the Former Prisoner of War: Life after Liberation,* published by Prototype Career Media, 1992. Kelnhofer himself was a former POW of the Japanese in World War II.

In 1983, the Department of Veterans Affairs devised a Prisoner of War Protocol Examination. Any POW who has not had this examination should do so. It is an excellent, thorough examination that covers many, many bases.

VITAMIN AND MINERAL DEFICIENCIES AND RESULTANT DISEASES
BY
DR. WILLIAM SHADISH, DECEMBER 2005

The vitamin deficiency diseases were among the most severe and deadly illnesses to affect POWs held by the Communist forces in North Korea. These deficiencies resulted from the absence of sufficient vitamins and nutrients in the diet. What we were given to eat in the early temporary camps and the permanent camps during the first year of our captivity was severely lacking in proteins, fats and vitamins, fruits and vegetables. Our food consisted solely of inadequate amounts of carbohydrates in the form of poorly cooked, often indigestible grains. For example, in Death Valley our ration was whole kernel, dried maize. Because it was only partially cooked, it appeared undigested in our post-consumption stools. After a few months of this diet, our weight loss was understandably rapid and extreme. Most prisoners quickly lost more than 40 percent of their body weight. Also suffering the ravages of dysentery, their emaciated bodies began to look like the victims of Buchenwald and Auschwitz.

As physicians we knew about and recognized the resultant dietary deficiency diseases. However, rarely were the extremes of these diseases to be found in the United States. Our patients in North Korea were the result of starvation conditions that included both primary malnutrition (a starvation diet) and secondary malnutrition (increased need and poor intestinal absorption), both of which were a planned part of the Chinese Communists' indoctrination program.

All vitamins are essential for health. There are four fat soluble vitamins: A, D, E, and K. They are poorly absorbed in malnutrition. The rest are water soluble vitamins.

FAT SOLUBLE VITAMINS:

Vitamin A: Found in meat, liver, fish, eggs, and butter, none of which we had. The deficiency diseases were night blindness, total blindness (rarely), vulnerability to infection, and poor skin health. Night blindness in the prison camps was severe and universal, and infections were rampant.

Vitamin D: Affects the absorption of calcium and phosphorus, essential in bone maintenance. Osteomalacia was the resultant disease, marked by a softening of the bones.

Vitamin E: An antioxidant found in meat, dairy products and vegetables, none of which made up our diet that first year. This result was muscle weakness, impaired vision, and impaired eye movements.

Vitamin K: A blood-clotting factor and involved in calcification of bone, especially seen in bleeding of the gums.

WATER SOLUBLE VITAMINS:

Vitamin B1 (Thiamine): Causes both dry and wet forms of beriberi. Essentially there are 3 syndromes, usually in sequence:

1. Polyneuropathy, dry beriberi—muscle weakness, sensory pain, and later sensory loss

2. Cardiovascular, wet beriberi—gives high output cardiac failure with markedly enlarged heart with thin walls and thrombi. Peripheral edema becomes massive. Often eventually results in cardiac death.

3. Korsakov syndrome—occurs late with psychotic like syndrome exhibiting confusion, apathy, and disorientation due to hemorrhaging in the central nervous system.

Vitamin B2 (Riboflavin): Causes cheilosis (cracking at the corners of the mouth with infection), stomatitis with glossitis, inflammation and atrophy of the tongue. Also causes eye changes with visual disturbance and corneal ulcers. Dermatitis also occurs with butterfly like patches on the face with skin atrophy.

Vitamin B5 (Niacin): Found in grains such as maize and sorghum, which we were fed much of the time, but often not absorbable. This deficiency causes pellagra, taught in the U.S. as "the three D disease": diarrhea, dermatitis, and dementia. In severe cases one can add the fourth D of death. Diarrhea was caused by ulceration of the bowel lining. Dermatitis, which was universal in the camps, was marked in exposed areas by redness, roughening, scaling fissures, and chronic fissures and inflammation in the mucous membranes of the mouth. Dementia was characterized by apathy and what was known as "the-face-the-wall syndrome."

Those so afflicted refused to eat, exercise, or leave their beds, and many of them suffered needless deaths that could have been prevented with a decent diet.

Vitamin C (ascorbic acid): Found in milk, animal products, fruits, and vegetables. Deficiency causes scurvy with hemorrhages and defects of healing. It is found in only the most deficient of diets, with hematomas of the gums and skin and bleeding into joints and intracerebral hemorrhage which often is fatal. One sees swelling of the gums, bleeding ulcers and secondary bacterial infections and wound infections. Healing is impaired and bleeding is severe enough to cause anemia.

Folate: Found in beans, nuts, and vegetables, but if cooked is destroyed. Deficiency causes megaloblastic anemia.

MINERALS ESSENTIAL TO GOOD HEALTH:

Zinc: Found in whole grains and fish. Deficiency causes diarrhea, poor appetite, poor wound healing, and altered immunity to diseases.

Selenium: Like Vitamin E, selenium is essential for hemoglobin. Deficiency causes muscle wasting (in China this is called Keshan Disease). If deficiency is severe cardiac wasting occurs.

Iron: Deficiency causes anemia.

Iodine: Deficiency causes hypothyroidism.

Copper: Deficiency causes muscle weakness.

Fluoride: Deficiency causes dental caries. Fluoride and Vitamin C deficiencies, along with severe gingival infections and ulcerations and breaking of teeth when biting on stones in the food, resulted in severe dental problems in the camps.

COLD WEATHER INJURIES: PREPARED FOR THE DEPARTMENT OF VETERANS AFFAIRS' NATIONAL ADVISORY COMMITTEE FOR FORMER PRISONERS OF WAR BY DR. WILLIAM SHADISH, WHO WAS A MEMBER OF THE COMMITTEE BETWEEN 1991–2000

A. ACUTE INJURY

Cold injury (frostbite) has been broken down into five different categories. First, second, third, and fourth degrees, and ill-classified conditions of the foot. These are varying intensities of the cold injury.

1) First-degree injury consists of the least injury, causing erythema and swelling of the extremity but without any blister formation or tissue loss.

2) Second-degree injury advances somewhat more with some whiteness of the skin and blister formation that contains clear fluid. This injury will go on eventually to heal without tissue loss.

3) Third-degree injury will cause gangrene of the superficial tissues, particularly skin loss in which one sees local gangrene and local necrosis. Bloody blisters are formed in the area of third-degree injury, indicating full-thickness loss. This will heal but with scar formation.

4) Fourth-degree injury is a complete necrosis of a segment or entire portion of a foot or hand, resulting in loss of the part; that is, loss of a toe, a finger, a hand, a foot, or ears.

5) The ill-classified condition of the foot is one that was first seen in Korea. It gives a hyperhidrosis with erythema and maceration without true frostbite. This occurs in temperatures above freezing over long periods of time. It is a diffuse, non-localized lesion.

Note: The first, second, third, and fourth degrees of frostbite occur in conditions below freezing. There are further classifications that are not significant for this purpose.

B. CHRONIC EFFECTS OF FROSTBITE INJURY

1) These effects will vary according to the intensity of the injury and can be seen at a late date after years of minor problems. These occur because of the addition of aging and loss of further vascularity from other processes; however, the process of frostbite has given a head-start in the vascular damage. Frostbite damages by destruction of the cells and particularly the intima of the small vessels thus decreasing the vascularity to the extremity.

2) First-degree frostbite, as noted, will leave very little in the way of physical signs. One can see some color change to the foot, particularly in the cold weather with whitening or bluish discoloration of the foot or hand or part that is involved. There is no scarring; there is no loss of part.

3) Second-degree frostbite will demonstrate the same signs, usually without scarring and without loss of part. However, the symptoms will be more marked. These include sensitivity to cold and very often hyperhidrosis. In addition, one will see almost invariably in frostbite of any degree, deformity of the nails with ridging and thickening of the nails either on single digits or on all of the digits. This is one of the signs that must be looked for and is very commonly found in frostbite residual disease.

4) Third-degree frostbite has caused skin loss and therefore one will see scarring in addition to the above symptoms. One will often see a bluish discoloration of the tips of the digits and notable sensitivity to cold and a hypersensitivity to irritation. Scarring will be present to some degree. Nail changes will be universal.

5) Fourth-degree frostbite residuals show, in addition to the above, evidence of loss of a part; most usually the great toe or the foot. The lower extremities are involved considerably more often than the upper extremities, perhaps in a ratio of seven to ten times on the lower extremity compared to the upper extremity. There will also be marked color changes, marked sensitivity to cold and actual joint pain with this type of injury. The skin will be roughened much as it would be in third-degree injury and, to some extent, in second-degree injury.

6) The ill-classified condition of the extremities shows a hyperhidrosis, some erythema and some maceration of the tissues in moist conditions. It is difficult to diagnose and does not fall to any category otherwise.

7) There is one test that is important to use and ranks with toenail deformity as a very significant sign of previous frostbite injury.

In doing this test, one grasps the great toe, or the next toe if the great toe is missing, with the thumb and two fingers and squeezes it tightly for three to five seconds to squeeze the blood out of the toe. One then releases it rapidly and times the return of blood flow to the toe.

The blood flow should return slowly, taking at least nine or ten seconds to return. If there has been cold injury, the blood vessel tone is basically gone and the flow will return rapidly so that any return of full color before eight or nine seconds in a toe should be considered definite evidence of late frostbite effect.

C. GENERAL COMMENTS

One must recall that cold injury occurs particularly in combat situations where the veteran was in a position to remain immobile for a considerable period of time, from two to twelve hours or more, depending also upon the intensity of the cold.

In addition, the footwear is a very important factor and should be queried by the examiner. Snowpacks (rubberized boots that do not allow perspiration to leave the boot) set up a moist atmosphere that adds to the susceptibility to cold injury. If one is in a position to move and walk, and to change socks regularly, the danger is minimized. However, in severe cold combat conditions and in prison camps, this is not possible. Therefore, anyone who was wearing the old type snowpacks in prolonged cold weather combat or prison camp experiences, and who demonstrates such symptoms as noted above, should be considered as having had cold injury with late residuals showing at this time. Although rubberized boots are the worst offenders, any type of combat boot can contribute to the development of this malady.

The cases of first or second degree frostbite and in ill-classified conditions of the foot, the physical signs may be minimal but the symptoms may be significant.[2] Hyperhidrosis is quoted often as a very significant factor but there are instances where this does not occur.

Marked changes of the nails, scarring, loss of parts, and rapid return of blood flow to the digits are the most significant factors in making the proper diagnosis.

Treatment is limited, using some form of ointment to help macerated and cracked skin, avoidance of cold weather and wearing of thick socks, changing them often. If there is loss of parts, special made shoes that are loose fitting may help.

ADDITIONAL COMMENTS[3]

The only way we had to treat frostbite was to cut off the toes that were black. Of course, prevention was the best thing. I tried to tell the combat soldiers how to prevent frostbite when they were on the front lines. I repeated this to the men after they were captured, and especially on the long march to the prison camps. The first thing in prevention was to keep your feet as dry as possible. When nightfall came and you were no longer fighting or marching, no matter how cold it was, you had to remove your boots and socks and dry them out for the next day. The second thing was to keep wiggling your toes and feet when they got cold so the blood would keep circulating. Unfortunately, on the long marches and in the temporary camps like Death Valley, the men were so sick, hungry, and exhausted that they simply did not have the energy to do this. And once their feet were actually frozen, there was nothing I could do for them. It was too late.

When I had to amputate, I used a knife made from the steel supports in our boots. Toes were not difficult to amputate. I would amputate them at what we called the line of demarcation and interphalangial joints. The toes had usually pretty much dried out up to that point so you could simply cut them off.

---

2.   Former Prisoners of War in the German POW camps and especially in the Korean POW camps were most exposed to these cold injuries due to lack of proper footwear, poor hygiene, and deliberate exposure to bitter cold by the enemy. Know also that cold weather foot gear was not issued to troops in Korea until after the bitterly cold winter of 1950 and spring of 1951.

3.   These comments emerged from an interview on March 18, 2004.

POST-TRAUMATIC STRESS DISORDER: AN ADDRESS DELIVERED BY DR. WILLIAM SHADISH AT A VETERANS ADMINISTRATION CONFERENCE ON PTSD IN AUGUST OF 1991 IN SAN FRANCISCO, CALIFORNIA[4]

Recently I was asked if I would come and speak with you concerning prison camp life, particularly in the Far East and most particularly that of the North Korean prisoner of war camps during the Korean War. I am qualified to speak on that because I was a prisoner there for 33 months.

During that time I was a physician, having just completed my internship and serving as a Battalion Surgeon with the 2nd Battalion of the 9th Infantry Regiment of the 2nd Division.

On December 1, 1950 our division was overrun by the Communist hordes and as a result, along with many others, I was captured.

It is important for you to know what happened in those prison camps in North Korea. Generally speaking this parallels very much the prison camps in Japan and Viet Nam and some of the prison camps in Europe, although the Europeans ex-prisoners of war on the average were not subjected to as severe a situation as those in the Far East. There are some-ex-prisoners of war from the European Theater who were indeed placed under severe conditions and these statements are not meant to diminish that fact.

It is important for you to know what happened so that you can better understand those ex-prisoners of war you are now examining, evaluating, and treating as your patients.

What does it mean to be a prisoner of war? What happens to the soul, the psyche, the mind during prolonged periods of starvation and brutality? What happens later when the soldier is liberated and released back into society?

How have they lived? What effect has their captivity experience had on their lives and their families?

---

4.   At the time of this address, Dr. Shadish was serving on the Veterans Administration's National Advisory Committee for Former Prisoners of War, a position he held between 1990—2000.

We know surprisingly little of the men and women who suffered so in the service of America. Few studies have been done and few articles written about their lives after returning home. In particular, we know little about their health, and the repercussions on the human body of starvation, disease, and injury left untreated over long periods of time.

So many POWs live in a world of silence, unable to tell others about their experiences. Some have never told their wives. Inherent in the POW psyche is a profound sense of shame and guilt for being captured, even when escape was not possible.

There is also survivor guilt to contend with, along with the memory of buddies who didn't make it, rage at their captors, and the long-term effects of a lifetime of psychic numbing. None of these feelings lessens over the years. Indeed, they intensify, creating a profound loss of power and self-esteem. Unexpressed, they can wreak havoc by coming out in insidious ways–alcoholism and drug abuse, spouse battering, child abuse, and even severe self-neglect and suicide.

I am certain it is difficult for you to understand what you are seeing now in these men in relation to their previous treatment as prisoners of war. When I talk with former prisoners of war I tell them, and they agree, that no matter how sympathetic health care workers are to them, if they were not prisoners of war in one of the Far Eastern camps, there is no way, and I repeat, no way others can really fully ever understand the situation that existed. However, many of you have tried so hard and are still trying. For that we are all grateful.

Perhaps I can help you understand a little bit more why the ex-POW is the way he is at this time. I will be talking particularly about the Korean ex-POWs. We have had the unusual experience of not only suffering physical hardships but also the severe mental stress of being the subject of intense indoctrination in an attempt to dislodge us from our democratic feelings, and place us in the ranks of the Communists. The Korean prison camps marked the first time that Communist captors began such mental indoctrinations, which again continued in the captivities of the men in Viet Nam prison camps.

Perhaps the best way I can do this is to try to outline briefly for you what happened during my 33 months as a prisoner. I will relate it to you from the viewpoint of a physician.

From the moment we were captured we began to realize that life would not be easy. I requested to remain with the wounded in my care but was taken away forcefully by the North Korean and Chinese captors. We were gathered together near the front lines for about 3 days and there heard for the first time about the "lenient treatment or policy" of the Communists. That is, if we went along and believed their indoctrination we would be treated leniently and if not we would be treated as war criminals. This theme was to be repeated and utilized during our entire confinement as POWs.

The next thing that happened to us, as happened with the Japanese ex-POWs, was the Death March. The march was from the front lines, with the wounded men attempting to keep up, with men becoming severely ill and debilitated with diarrhea and dysentery (there was no water to drink and we were forced to drink out of rice paddies that were fertilized with human feces). As we marched for 22 days, we tried to carry as many of our men as we could. But there was a limit to what we could carry and those who could not continue fell out and either were shot or left to freeze to death in the terribly cold winter of 1950. The temperatures in those high mountains near the Manchurian border reached 40 and 50 below zero. We had not been prepared with clothing for those conditions. Many had no footwear since it was taken from them by the Communists to use. Those who did keep their footwear found that their boots soon wore out and frostbite of the feet occurred almost immediately. When you hear complaints that a man had frostbite and his toes get numb in cold weather, or he is missing toes, you know there was a valid reason for him having those symptoms.

The wounded were forced to walk along with the rest of us, being supported as best was possible. Some had festering wounds which had to be allowed to heal expectantly since we had no equipment and no medication. I am not saying we had a little; we had NO medication.

Food was almost nonexistent. A small bowl of boiled, hard corn kernels was given once or twice a day. It was of course not sufficient to maintain body weight, particularly under the trying conditions of marching 12 hours and 20 miles or more a night over icy roads. Consequently, one began to see emaciation and all the early signs of vitamin deficiencies.

The second phase of that severe winter began Christmas Day 1950 on our arrival at the first temporary camp, a camp that was aptly called Death Valley. And it was Death Valley. I was then one of two physicians in the camp. We were allowed to minister to the sick as well as we could. That consisted of emotional support, lancing of boils with knives made from the instep metal of our combat boots and boiling of hot water for them for some form of liquid replacement from the severe diarrhea which was now rampant and universal in the camp.

In this 3-month period from December into early March, we began to see the outbreak of lobar pneumonia.

I remember my professor in medical school telling us in 1944 how fortunate we were that we would never see pneumonia without penicillin. Well, it didn't work out that way for me; I did see pneumonia without penicillin. And I will say to you how fortunate you will be never to see pneumonia without the antibiotics we now have. These men would develop consolidation of their lungs and rapidly within 2 to 3 days begin to get dusky with cyanosis and eventually have cardiac arrests. It was almost universally fatal. Remember, these are emaciated men with protein and vitamin deficiencies, with no reserves to assault severe illnesses without antibiotics.

At this point we were able eventually to persuade the Communists to give us some medications. We were given sulfadiazine tablets. A Chinese officer would walk with us amongst the prisoners; we would point out the pneumonia cases and we would be given one sulfa tablet for each. We had about 40 patients; that meant we had enough sulfa to actually be effective in five men.

One of my most difficult tasks was to determine which 5 men I felt would be salvageable with the sulfa and which men would be the most helpful to the other men in camp if they survived. Those men got the medication; not one per person.

Diarrhea at that time was universal and severely weakened the men. They were jammed into the rooms and not allowed to be let out to go to the bathroom. As a result they soiled themselves over and over. The stench in the rooms was overwhelming. Of course, the germs spread from one to another.

The men who could go out of the rooms to relieve themselves would soil the ground with feces. Fortunately, this would freeze. However, by late February it appeared as though when the thaw came we would really be in trouble. There was no water to wash with, only enough to drink and to cook. I did not wash or cut my hair or shave for a period of 6 months.

The lice infected us to the point of almost driving us crazy. We picked lice off of one another daily.

In January the majority of the men in Death Valley were sent on to one of the permanent camps on the Yalu River, at the border between Manchuria and Korea. Several hundred of the men remaining were sick and wounded, too ill to go. I asked for and was given permission to remain with them and did so until the first part of March when we began a second march from that camp to the Yalu River. This was accomplished in a period of 7 nights and my impression was that we marched about 100 to 130 miles.

Men who were severely jaundiced from hepatitis, men who were exhausted from dysentery, men who had infected wounds were to march these 7 nights to the next camp.

Incidentally, we were marched at night only because they were greatly fearful of American Air Force attacks.

When we arrived at Camp 5, I was placed with the enlisted men as the only physician for approximately 2500 to 3000 men. The other officers had been separated from them.

I was allowed to hold a sick call. This time I had some medication, a powder for diarrhea called tannalbin which really was a charcoal, and occasional sulfadiazine tablets. I was given one small child type dental forceps with which I pulled many, many rotten teeth, some with and most without anesthesia. The men's teeth hurt so bad they could no longer eat, and if they could not eat the swill we were fed, they would soon die.

It was bad enough to eat the food they fed us which included sorghum, millet, or corn, practically never any protein, never any eggs, meat, or milk. When we were fed sorghum, pellagra and vitamin deficiencies appeared.

About this time we began to see the advanced, severe effects of vitamin deficiencies, which included both the wet and dry forms of beriberi and pellagra. Everyone had aching legs and feet from neuritis. Most people were edematous from tissue damage. Many had outright beriberi heart disease or at least respiratory distress. A great number died from this form of congestive heart failure.

In pellagra we saw the 3 Ds: diarrhea, dermatitis, and dementia. You have all learned about these. The dementia caused apathy. This is what was termed (for lack of better words) "give-up-itis" or "face-to-the-wall syndrome." It was not "give-up-itis." These terribly sick men, who had lost half of their body weight, no longer cared about anything and turned their faces to the wall and died. They did not die because they gave up; they died because they had apathy caused by severe pellagra.

With the spring and summer came malaria, which was endemic in camp. There was dengue fever, scurvy, and many other curses of illness that could be thrown upon mankind in deprived conditions.

Incidently, you must realize that all of these things did not occur by chance. This was purposeful deprivation, humiliation and degradation, forced upon these men so they would live lower than animals and thus were more susceptible to be persuaded to accept the "lenient policy" of Communism and to cooperate with their Communist captors.

I want to tell you here and now that these men did not denounce America, except for a handful. They stood behind their country and fought their enemy as best they could. As a matter of fact, contrary to what some psychiatrists and psychologists, such as Mayer and Kinkead say, there was less collaboration in the

Korean POW camps than in any previous wars, in spite of the greater mental pressure put upon these men to cooperate.

The Chinese permitted me to remain with the enlisted men, treating them as best I could with minimal supplies, until July 1951 at which time they brought in their own "barefoot doctors" who had been trained about 3 months in medicine. I was removed to the officers camp. I was no longer allowed to see or treat any of those men, although we continued treating the officers as best we could.

◆　　　◆　　　◆

Now to relate all of this to what you are seeing in survivors today. First of all, you can see Post-Traumatic Stress Disorder in these men. From what I saw as a physician in prison camp, there is no question but that everyone of us has PTSD to at least a moderate if not fairly severe degree. The stress was not brief. It was constant, for years in severe degrees.

It is distressing to see a physical exam in these records stating, "The patient comes in well dressed, conversant, and appearing very normal."

That is what you see and that is what he wants you to see. But if you want to know what kind of a life that man lives, what his residual signs and symptoms are as a result of his POW experience, talk to his wife. Ger her in. You will find a totally different story from what he tells you. His PTSD prevents him from discussing any health problem normally.

You have to understand one thing: that in order to survive in a POW camp where the enemy has total control over you, one must shelter himself as much as possible. One cannot lose his temper and attack the enemy because it would lead to sudden and certain death. He learns to control his anger, his rage, and he must do it by building a shell around himself and crawling into it every time a stressful incidence occurred–and they occurred daily. Someone aptly said, "Life in a prison camp in the Far East is composed of long periods of boredom punctuated by brief moments of sheer terror." Therefore, these men had learned to "clam up" or pull into their shells to withdraw from the world they knew and avoid further punishments. They learned this the hard way, as a matter of life and death over a period of years. They learned it well and used it constantly. When they came home, this learned and conditioned behavior could not be abandoned. Ask the wives about this; they will tell you, "He is impossible to reach; he is emotionally numb."

I am fortunate. I am married to a wonderful woman who has taught me to come out of that shell. At first when a stressful situation came around, I withdrew. I would not speak to her. I would not speak to anyone, which is a very abnormal way of behavior in such situations. Karen has drawn me out of that shell. I find myself tending to slip back into those behavior patterns from time to time, but I can at least see it now and can work against it. But many of the men don't have that kind of support, understanding, and guidance. It takes a lot of patience and practice and commitment on the part of wives and husbands to be overcome. It may take a lot of work with a therapist as well. Many men respond best to support groups found in V.A. Medical Centers throughout the country, and there are also wives' support group that are equally effective. Many ex-POWs are cursed with that shell and are resistant to ridding themselves of it. They don't even understand fully that this type of behavior is abnormal or acknowledge that they actually behave this way. It took me, a physician, 20 years to recognize this problem in myself.

When the ex-POW is asked how he feels, he will probably respond that he is "fine" and has no problems. If asked if he has any problems with the aftereffects of prison camp, he will say, "No, I'm doing well." You see, it's that conditioning again not to complain or admit any weakness. Talk to their wives. I have talked to these men. They have written to me. Their wives have written me. You can believe me, they have PTSD badly and they need you. They need to talk about it; they need support groups, or whatever method it takes to make them aware of this behavior and be willing to work on it.

Yes, these men may be functioning reasonably well, but how much better would they have functioned had they not had this experience in their lives?

We find that when this man was working at his job, he was able to cope day by day. He became a workaholic, using his work as an alcoholic might to cope with his job, drinking only in the evening. Alcohol use is or was very prevalent in this group of veterans. It was hard, but the busier he kept the easier it was to cope, to continue his learned behavior and to not think about things being different with him than with an average person, or even an average veteran.

But wait until that man reaches his retirement age and he suddenly doesn't have that all-consuming job. We find (in every part of the country) that this time in life often precipitates an acute exacerbation of problems in these men (increased nightmares on retirement).

Ask these men about anger; ask these men about their nightmares and waking up in a sweat with pounding hearts and feelings of terror; ask these men about their ability to communicate; ask these men about their pattern of problem-solving; ask them about periods of depression, mood swings, destructive habits. Ask them all these questions. Draw them out. They must be drawn out. Most will resist or not tell you about things voluntarily. This is particularly true for the Korean group because not only were they treated badly in the prison camps, but they were treated badly when they came home. Remember, this is the first war the United States did not win outright. We had to negotiate. And the American people didn't want to talk about that. So unlike the recent Gulf War, there were no big "Heroes Welcome!" signs for these men who had so bravely suffered under unspeakable conditions in unspeakable ways.

Instead, they were vilified by people like Mayer and Kinkead who reported they were all collaborators. It was not until Al Biderman came along with his book *March to Calumny* that this cloud was dispelled. However, in the interim all of the records of the Korean ex-POWs were tagged, "No favorable action." That tag remained until the examinations and trials were over, a period of 5 years for some in which they lost all promotions or other favorable action. In addition, they received ne medals for what they had done. Compare that to the returned POWs from Viet Nam who were told by their officers, "If you are being forced or tortured for information or to do things against your will, hold off for as long as you can, but do what you must under duress in order to survive; you will not be punished." As a matter of fact, the 766 returning Viet Nam POWs received more than 2000 medals.

The former POWs from Korea are bitter and I think understandably bitter. They have a right to be bitter. They don't trust anyone and they will resist trusting you. That is why I repeat again and again, draw them out, get them in a group session, get their wives involved. They need it badly.

Medically speaking they are also being hurt now. There are many presumptive illnesses, defined by act of Congress, of which you are no doubt aware. However, the interpretations of these conditions and illnesses are not being done appropriately. Take for instance traumatic osteoarthritis. If one had suffered a broken hip or a dislocated shoulder, one can prove this by x-ray to the Veterans Administration and the diagnosis of traumatic osteoarthritis will be accepted by them as a treatable and compensable disease entity with service connection. However, what about the many, many minor traumas these men suffered such as falling on the ice every few yards for days during the marches? How about the beatings administered by guards? How about carrying heavy telephone poles with 3 or 4 other men until one might slip and fall, causing the pole to fall on the others' shoulders? How about consideration of men with no muscle tissue to support their spines carrying heavy loads with multiple microtrauma on cartilaginous surfaces? Why would that not lead to traumatic arthritis later? The V.A. doesn't accept this. They say there is no literature to support this.

Let's go to beriberi heart disease. We all know that beriberi heart disease can cause death, and it has now been proven that the deficiency caused condition does not spare the heart; the muscle fibers degenerate as well as those of other muscles. However, beriberi is a disease of the nervous system. We know that. Why then is it so difficult to assume that the perkinje fibers in the heart are also affected and that is why so many ex-POWs develop arrhythmia later in life? These many not have been present early in the disease, but as nature takes her toll with age these men have a lower threshold than the average person for developing heart disease. However, the V.A. does not accept beriberi heart disease as causing arrhythmia later because "there is nothing written in the literature about this being a cause." [Note: This causation has recently been accepted by the Veterans Administration]

And, indeed, there is nothing in the literature. I have researched it and many others have researched it. The problem is that in this country we have never seen beriberi heart disease and the deprivations to cause it like was seen in the prison camps. There was not enough of it around to be seen or written about and thus documented in a formal literary manner to the satisfaction of those making medical and compensatory decisions. Because of this, these former POWs must pay the price of being told that their medical conditions are not related to their POW experiences; they are told they are just getting old, even if it is sooner than the average veteran.

One can go on and on and on with examples such as these, of what has happened to these men and what is happening now. Many, many are the instances of compensation denied, even in the face of "buddy statements" that the men were led to believe would help and went to a lot of difficulty to obtain.

But what I am really here to tell you is that you are the ones who can help these men. If these ex-POWs come in for a Protocol Examination, it is imperative that the physician who sees them examines them thoroughly, asked them questions, draws them out, speaks to the family members, and then makes the diagnoses. And taking into account what has happened to these men before, the doctor must then make a statement (if it appears appropriate) that it appears that their present problems are due to or related to the severe deprivations and calamities inflicted on them when they were prisoners of war. Only if this is on a man's record will the Adjudication Board consider this to be a compensable and treatable disease that is service connected. I can tell you, if you do not put this on the record, it will not be considered by the Board. So you are vital to helping these men who have each gone through his own hell and come back. They need your help; they look to you for help; expect them to be hostile; expect them to have trouble with anger and distrust; expect them to be reserved and to deny things unless drawn out. Remember, it is not you they are reacting to; it is the echoes of those dark days, the conditioned responses they learned as survival techniques; it is the rage in their souls that they have been unable to let out all their lives. If you can understand these things, if you can put up with them and give them some way to help themselves as well as treat them for their medical conditions, you will do so much more for them than has been done before. They are all great men and they need you!

WILLIAM SHADISH LETTER TO THE U.S. SENATE INTERNAL SECURITY SUBCOMMITTEE, NOVEMBER 9, 1954

Mr. Louis Columbo
Senate Office Building
Room 41
Internal Security Subcommittee
Washington, D.C.

Dear Lou:

In reply to your request, I am submitting the following list of recommendations which I consider important to counteract any attempt at indoctrination of captured American personnel by Communists at any future time.

1. The most important factor in my consideration is the basic knowledge of the individual concerning both our government and that of the Communists. This is something which appears impossible for the Army alone to insure. It must begin in the home and school at an early age. From my observation, those men in prison with me were, in many instances, almost totally deficient of a working knowledge of their own government, much less that of the enemy. Therefore, their verbal and mental battle against indoctrination was fought with rather poor equipment and with poor results. This can only be corrected by concentration of effort to improve the working knowledge of all citizens in regard to this democracy of ours. Another important factor seems to be the apathy with which a large number of Americans view the menace of Communism. Perhaps in this aspect, it would be helpful to suggest that a selected group of individuals, including former prisoners of war of the Communists, and any other individual who has had first hand knowledge of their aims and methods, be utilized to disseminate this information and bring the point closer to home.

2. As far as the individual soldier in service is concerned, a specific affirmation of code of conduct must be established and clearly explained to each and every individual. Included in this should be first and foremost, the statement that regardless of status as a prisoner, the soldier is bound by oath to remain a soldier

and no statement or action to the contrary by the enemy can in any way change this. Often the enemy would attempt to convince the soldiers that they were no longer a part of the U.S. Army but were "liberated". A number of men appeared not to understand the implications here. Had they previously been told precisely their duty, I feel the outcome would have been different. Of course it was known that they remained a soldier, but it had not been emphasized forcefully enough.

3. The knowledge of the tactics of the enemy of singling out the "leaders", the highest ranking officials, and punishing them for any attempt at retention of organization or discipline must be noted. Here again emphasis on the duty of the officer must be forcefully restated. There will always be casualties among the highest ranks but this will be the cost of preservation of organization. A notable instance of this was the preservation of organization among the Turkish men and officers. They significantly suffered less as a whole because of this. Those units whose organizational breakdown was most complete suffered most both physically and mentally.

4. Lastly, a statement as to physical preparedness seems unnecessary. However, I would like to emphasize the fact that the prisoners will in the future, at the most, be allowed to retain the barest amount of clothing possible. For this reason concentration should be made to devise clothing for combat troops which are of sufficient warmth and strength to maintain him in cold climates. This clothing should preferably be the innermost garments which he most probably can be allowed to retain.

Lou, I hope this is what Senator Jenner and Mr. Mendell wish. If I can be of any more help please let me know. The copy of the proceedings of the Powell case will be sent to you under separate cover. Thanks for sending it to me.

Sincerely yours,

William R. Shadish, Maj, MC

ABOUT THE AUTHORS

William Shadish is a retired plastic surgeon who spent twenty years in the U.S. Army. He served as a combat physician during the Korean War before being captured in 1950. After liberation and his return to active duty in the States in 1953, he specialized in plastic, reconstructive, and hand surgery. Following his army retirement in 1966, he went into private practice in Redding, California, from which he retired in 1992. Today, he and his wife Karen care for their prize-winning roses and an extensive fossil collection.

Lewis H. Carlson is a retired professor of history and director of American Studies at Western Michigan University. Among his eleven books are *Remembered Prisoners of a Forgotten War: An Oral History of Korean War POWs* and *We Were Each Other's Prisoners: An Oral History of World War II American and German Prisoners of War*. With his wife Simone, he lives in Austin, Texas, and Ludington, Michigan.

978-0-595-46899-7
0-595-46899-3

2683250